the garden of
equal delights

the garden of equal delights

the practice and principles of forest gardening

Anni Kelsey

tp

Triarchy Press

Published in this first edition in 2020 by:

Triarchy Press
Axminster, UK

www.triarchypress.net

A catalogue record for this book is available from the British Library.

ISBNs:
Print: 978-1-911193-74-6
ePub: 978-1-911193-75-3
pdf: 978-1-911193-76-0

Printed by TJ International Ltd., Padstow, Cornwall

Triarchy Press

*It is not from ourselves
that we will learn to be better than we are.*

~ Wendell Berry ~

for Emmi, Pip, Amelie, Luke, Vinnie,
Amber and Alexandra

contents

foreword

Anni Kelsey's *Garden of Equal Delights* inspires and challenges you to think differently, not only about how to garden, but also how to live. Although Anni introduces forest gardening through a rich narrative of practical experiences as she transforms her own garden into a productive and beautiful space, she also gently introduces the personal act of forest gardening as a metaphor for managing wider relationships. For Anni, forest gardening is the middle ground between completely letting go, and imposing with mechanical precision exactly what happens.

In her deeply engaging book, she introduces you to the practice of forest gardening as a way that maximises the productivity and regenerative capacity of the whole person-garden relationship, not through constant intervention, but through giving the plants (and animals) in the garden high levels of autonomy and freedom to find what is healthiest for the whole. Her principles of forest gardening turn the table on our current obsession with frantic and exhausting action and micro-management. Instead, her emphasis is on building an intimate relationship with one's environment through contemplative observation, so that an intervention only occurs at the right time, with minimal effort, so as to produce maximum impact in the long-term.

In this time of over-consumption, burn-out and environmental crisis, Anni's *Garden of Equal Delights* provides the practical foundations for transforming your garden – and yourself.

Dr Andrea Berardi
Senior Lecturer in Environmental Information Systems
The Open University, UK

preface

A forest garden is a different garden that needs to be gardened differently by a different gardener.

This book is first and foremost about forest gardening as an interactive and co-creative engagement between forest garden and forest gardener – about fundamental principles to guide this ongoing interaction. Planning and planting a forest garden is just the very beginning of the relationship and this co-creativity begins immediately after planting and continues ever after.

First, there is the everyday level of interacting with the forest garden to support it in creating and sustaining an ecosystem that will become healthy, fertile and abundant. But there is a deeper level as well which is about how we habitually relate to the natural world. This is the story of the remaking of our human perceptions from a perspective of assumed and rightful dominance and control of nature to a place of humble, appreciative, thoughtful and sensitive integration with it. Therein are significant treasures that are not at all obvious from the outset.

My motivation and intention for writing this book have been to share what I have learned from my own gardens. I hope that it will enable forest gardeners and would-be forest gardeners to set out consciously on the polyculture path to the heart of their gardens.

Anni Kelsey

introduction

A forest garden is like no other garden. As well as food harvests and many tangible benefits for the land and local ecology, forest gardening presents the gardener with an opportunity to find a new relationship with the natural world, to see, feel and think differently; even to live differently.

A forest garden is a beautiful, fertile, healthy and abundant edible landscape. It is first conceived in the gardener's imagination, it gestates in our planning and planting and then one day it is ready to grow. But we don't plant a forest garden and then garden it just as if it was a 'normal' horticultural garden. We garden it differently because it is a different garden.

As an ecosystem a forest garden is able to generate its own health, fertility and abundance, and the 'work' of the emerging and maturing ecosystem is done entirely by the natural world. However, having said that, a forest garden is human-inspired and a place that has a human purpose, and the forest gardener will always have a pivotal and vital role in gently guiding and supporting it. The forest gardener's essential task is to learn what that means in practical terms. My aim is to show that there are no hard and fast rules about interacting with a forest garden; there is no timetable of annual activities, just an ongoing relationship in which we decide as sensitively as we can what to do and when.

I set out to write this book because I wanted to understand and then share what I had learned about the dynamics of forest gardening. There are already very good books about how to design, plan and plant a forest garden, but I am not aware of any books about what comes next – about the role of the forest gardener in the actual gardening of the forest garden – what to do or what not to do.

I fell in love with the idea of an abundant, edible, easily maintained garden one summer's afternoon. Then I fell in love with my own transforming garden over the following years as I gradually learned that a forest garden is a different garden that needs to be gardened differently by a different gardener. I also came to realise that forest gardens are about personal change and healing – healing for the garden and for the gardener. I found out that seeing things differently and acting differently in the garden translated into seeing and acting differently out of the garden, and in effect meant a new way of being.

Writing this book has been a process of unfurling: a journey from the knowledge I knew I had gained but which was locked up inside me. Finding a way of explaining and exploring that knowledge, and sharing it as clearly as possible, has been delightfully simple and very complex. Virtually everything within it has been learned directly from my two small forest gardens but this learning has been framed by the context of ecological theory about how ecosystems work in the real world. It is as close as I can get to nature's message to us gardeners.

As I thought about the potential content of the book it quickly became obvious that I had very much taken to heart the maxim of Masanobu Fukuoka[1] to do the minimum in my garden. Alongside this I had learned a huge amount about the ecological processes by which a forest garden works from Dave Jacke and Eric Toensmeier's two books on edible forest gardening. The central theme of a forest garden is that it is designed to be or to become an ecosystem. *Everything* that happens thereafter relates directly to this. Each activity undertaken in the garden – or more likely not undertaken – has a significant impact for better or worse on this ecosystem, and it is vital to understand the dynamics of these interactions. And so I set out to watch and understand my own interactivity with my forest garden – my garden of equal delights – and to seek an understanding of the relationship I had developed with my garden. I knew I had begun with a basic understanding about ecosystems, about biodiversity and about health and fertility which was the foundation for everything else. And then I realised that I was using what amounted to a set of assumed or intuited, almost subconscious,

---

[1] Masanobu Fukuoka (1913-2008) was a Japanese farmer who dedicated his life to finding a natural way of farming, looking always for simplicity and for tasks he could leave not done.

principles that guided both what I did in the garden and what I left undone.

The principles are set out in chapter 4 and explained in detail in the subsequent chapters. They demonstrate that by binding action (and non-action) firmly to ecological realities and biological processes the forest gardener is able to fit into a quasi-natural system in which we are unquestionably not the leader, but just one of very many co-participants.

This is of vital importance because in becoming forest gardeners we are stepping away from everything being about what we – as individuals or as a race – want. Becoming a forest gardener is no small thing, but it does require us to become smaller, shrinking to occupy a more fitting and appropriate ecological niche than the place we formerly occupied. Thus we start to learn that this is not about imposing our will on the garden, but paradoxically neither is it about letting nature get on with it alone. Rather this is about effectively pressing the pause button on human intervention and entering into an interaction or a dialogue with the natural processes at play in the garden. Although the concept of giving up control is a simple one this is a profound and challenging change of direction.

Crucially, this is completely different to the role of a conventional horticultural gardener who is used to specific 'how to' instructions; instead principles guide forest gardeners towards the knowledge, insight and understanding that enable us to work out the 'how to' for our own garden. By giving up control and replacing it with trust, by watching and waiting and doing only the minimum, forest gardeners set out on the polyculture path. This is a way of being that unlocks how to be at peace with the wider world and how to allow things to work in harmony with nature and with life. There is no proper way, no right way – the only way is the 'get stuck in and work it through for yourself' way. Your way will not be the same as my way – because you are not me, I am not you. As our insight deepens into the complexities of nature unfolding within the garden, we travel ever further along this polyculture path towards the heart of the garden. And, over time, both forest garden and forest gardener proceed together towards a place of love, healing and beauty and, as forest gardeners, we emerge from our polyculture cocoon to realise that we have gained a different relationship to, and appreciation of, the natural world.

This book began as a collection of fragments of insight, hastily scribbled down as they dropped into my consciousness, and which, with more thought, unfurled into a set of principles. I have taken *lots* of time to mull them over, interrogate my thinking and to constantly assess and reassess precisely how they have been derived from past experience and how they inform my ongoing interaction with the garden. Eventually the principles crystallised into their final form and as I followed the thinking that supported them I found their intersections and interconnections, their own relatedness. I could see them as part of a greater whole, each one distinct but all inextricably linked; a robust network of mutually supporting ideas and practices. Because of these interconnections it was not easy to come to a logical arrangement of the material I want to share in this book. So I have chosen to present the principles of forest gardening woven in alongside the story of my developing forest garden and my own development as a forest gardener.

So this is my story and my garden's story too. This is a story about letting go and learning, about not seeking but finding, and an account of a further journey beyond the basics of starting a forest garden into the more hidden complexities of how it ticks, and exploring more fully what working with nature might actually mean (if indeed it means anything). It is about why and how I chose to reject control and to trust in nature and about spending a lot of time watching and waiting, learning to stop do-do-doing all the time and about delighting in abundance without having to possess or claim it all. It is about humbly and patiently learning from the garden and from the wider natural world and how I thereby gained what I call polyculture eyes, polyculture mind and a polyculture heart. How I journeyed on a path of unfolding insight, connectedness and ever-increasing trust; and how that opened up into respect, reverence, awe, joy, delight and ultimately into love. It is about learning to travel on a path of co-creation with nature – on an ever-closer journey from separation towards integration with – or embeddedness in – the garden and the natural world.

Planting and tending a forest garden is a unique invitation to reject our cultural norm of dominance and control of the natural world and of bending it to our human wills. It is also about how we become nature's apprentices because it is our own direct learning of nature's language and meanings that will make us forest gardeners. Forest gardening then, is about entering into a new covenant with the land and with the natural world, healing the garden and the landscape and thereby ultimately to bring some measure of inner healing to ourselves.

> *The ultimate goal of forest gardening is not only the growing of crops, but also the cultivation and perfection of new ways of seeing, of thinking and of acting in the world.*
>
> ~ Jacke & Toensmeier

Whilst this book is specifically about forest gardens and forest gardening, I think that it has wider implications. Every one of us, at this point in time, needs to consider carefully our own role in contributing to the poor health of our planet. The deeper message that emerges on the polyculture journey of forest gardening – of relinquishing control of the natural world and joining with it in genuine co-operation – has the potential for much wider application beyond the boundaries of any garden.

Throughout this book I have used the terms garden/er and forest garden/er as more or less synonymous. Sometimes I use 'nature' and sometimes 'life' but I mean the same by both words. My name for my garden – the garden of equal delights – is part of emphasising that what we usually experience as distinct and separate parts, and as hierarchies, are simply equal aspects of unity.

Whilst writing this I was very inclined to use the pronouns 'she' or 'her' to describe nature and the natural world. However I am, of course, mindful of the wisdom of avoiding gendered language and I have therefore written about nature and the natural world as 'it'. However this gives me a certain amount of discomfort because it de-personalises what I am attempting to describe. Not that I consider nature to be a person, but clearly *it* is alive and it was this aliveness that I really had wanted to capture. So please bear with me and with the constraints that language imposes upon any writer – and allow me to emphasise that the longer my association with the natural world, the deeper my appreciation, respect and awe for *its* inherent vitality and wisdom.

tribute to all gardeners

Throughout this book I describe a forest gardener as a different gardener. I talk about relinquishing control and even responsibility and I describe many horticultural methods and norms in apparently harsh terms. It is absolutely not my intention to criticise gardeners who, in the ways we have always known, create beauty, grow food and look after nature.

My late Uncle Fred was a wonderful, kind, gentle, caring man who spent his ninety plus years mostly out of doors caring for the thousands of plants in his garden and plant nursery. When I think of him I can still see the soft smile on his face, I recall the fruit swelling on the wonderful old trees in the orchard and I can almost smell the tomatoes in one glass house and the carnations in the other. His influence is firmly written into my childhood and I remember him with great love and affection.

Yet even kind and gentle Uncle Fred was to some degree destructive to the local environment in and around his garden and greenhouses. He was because we all are and, hard as it may be to come to recognise and accept it, even the best intentioned of our interactions in the garden are actually often harsh and controlling. We are not responsible for the heritage we have been handed by our culture, but it is time to learn new ways direct from nature as it manifests in the forest garden and beyond.

part one

a different garden

a different garden

*A forest garden is a different garden that needs to be
gardened differently by a different gardener*

Let's begin with my definition of a forest garden:

**A forest garden is both a planned landscape and a
functioning ecosystem that takes its composition, form and
structure from a natural woodland. It is a naturalistic
landscape, but not an entirely natural or wild one. Humans
are an integral part of a forest garden but they must accept
and learn their own place within the ecosystem.**

There are so many things to like about a forest garden. To begin
with it is an edible cornucopia that produces an abundance of all
kinds of fruits and vegetables throughout the year. It is enduringly
productive as many plants live for years or are able to reproduce
themselves without help from the gardener, therefore very few (if
any) need to be replanted or re-sown from year to year. A forest
garden needs much less work than a traditional vegetable or fruit
garden or allotment. Digging, weeding, fertilising and pest control
are not required at all and (at least in a cool temperate climate)
watering is a very rare occurrence. Despite this lack of gardening
work, a forest garden is a healthy environment and one that is able
to continually improve its soil fertility and thereby its productivity.

Forest gardens are also about much more than food as they can
produce many other valuable products based on trees and plants –
wood for everything from building materials to poles, posts and
fences to craft work; fibrous plants can yield tying and basketry
materials; and other plants can be used to prepare herbal medicines,
personal care products, coloured dyes and more. There are also
options to breed plants suited to particular circumstances, or to
collect whole plant families, or to use Stephen Barstow's approach
and grow 'edimental' plants – that is plants more commonly known

as ornamentals, but which are in fact edible as well. There is infinite scope for personalising each forest garden – anyone thinking about growing a forest garden will not be lost for possibilities to dream of or plan for.

And there are other personal, human benefits. Forest gardens are special places in themselves, the antithesis of modern life – harmonious, integrated, beautiful, relaxed and gentle – a healthful and plenteous unity, full of delight. They make a lovely setting for many personal and social uses – quiet places to retreat to, social and educational gatherings, etc.

A forest garden looks different to conventional gardens. It is a visually complex, joyous mixture of edibles and floral plants that is neither cottage garden, kitchen garden, or allotment. It is at times stunningly beautiful but at other times it can be aesthetically challenging when wild plants are allowed to stay or when the needs of the ecosystem mean that the gardener allows the garden to become somewhat messy.

A forest garden is able to generate so many wonderful attributes precisely because it is an ecosystem[2]. Yes, it has a particular composition, structure and planting pattern but, after the initial planting of the garden, what makes it work is the fact that it is an ecosystem – a simple one to begin with, but growing in complexity and resilience all the time. A forest garden that is gardened in a conventional way cannot function as intended. This fact is paramount.

This being the case, the long term task of tending a forest garden requires a gardener who is informed about natural processes, who understands the systems they are embedded in and who, crucially, is able to stand back and restrain their human impulse to control, and to undertake the journey of learning to co-operate and to co-create with nature. The forest gardener becomes the vital facilitator of this ecosystem. Without their sensitive attention and interaction, it

---

[2] A forest garden is not and cannot be a re-creation of nature, but it can function in an eco-systemic way and thereby link to and draw upon the natural processes of life.

would revert to a totally wild space, which might not be such a bad thing *per se*, but would not be the purpose of the garden. Conversely, if the continual interventions of conventional horticulture are meted out on a forest garden, the ecosystem will never be permitted to develop its own complex integrity and resilience. In other words, to achieve such a radically different type of garden you also need a radically different type of gardener: one who can learn how to slip inside nature's own skin – at first learning from nature and, over time, increasingly becoming one with nature.

Later chapters will explain these individual but interconnected aspects of forest gardening. Each is a single aspect of a unity and they stand or fall together – remove or ignore one of them and everything will start to fall apart as the ecosystem unravels. Because we don't know best, nature does.

I remember so vividly the day in July 2005 when I first read about forest gardening. I had experienced a bit of a eureka moment in my own garden earlier that afternoon as I idly wondered whether there could possibly be such a thing as a self-maintaining perennial food garden. From that time onwards I have been intrigued, excited, fascinated and utterly absorbed by forest gardens and forest gardening.

Because the forest gardener is so crucial to the ongoing development and wellbeing of the forest garden, I have given a great deal of thought to how this relationship of garden and gardener can be adequately described and conveyed. I began my first forest garden with a set of precepts listed below that guided my interaction with that garden:

*   No digging
*   No walking on the soil
*   No chemical fertilisers or weed killers or pesticides
*   No importing or exporting fertility – nothing is brought into the garden to add fertility and all the plant material generated on site is used within the garden
*   Get the maximum output of edible harvests for the minimum input of time and effort

Over the years I learned a way of being with the garden that turned into more of a dance with nature than anything that resembled the conventional gardening I had done before. Eventually I settled on a set of principles (see chapter 4) that could be used to guide this delicate relationship; principles that were sufficiently general to be applicable to virtually any scenario and sufficiently specific to be a practical guide in the decision-making process.

could any garden be a forest garden?

A woodland ecosystem is the inspiration and model for forest gardens, and they can be planted in a space of any size – as large or as small as you like or need – as long as the climate, soil and landforms are suitable. But in places that are not suited to a woodland ecosystem it is equally possible to model a garden on a different type of ecosystem, for example moorland, heathland or coast. I cannot say for certain, but because there is great emphasis on watching and waiting before taking decisions, based on what you see happening, I anticipate that many of the principles for forest gardens could be applicable to other contexts as well.

how does the forest garden?

In the early summer of 2017 I was on a camping holiday in rural France. I pulled my chair into the shade at the campsite and sat down to write about forest gardens for this book. It was a scorching hot June day and I was glad of the shade of the tall oaks. I had already noticed many small and medium height sweet chestnut trees in the area immediately around our camping pitch and as I peered into the shade of the trees through the bright summer sun I thought I could see alder trees. I got up to check the leaves, and yes, they were alders. Close to my chair at the edge of the woodland were ferns, brambles and a mixture of wild herbaceous plants and flowers. A nearby tree stump was clothed with honeysuckle. Having sat down with the intention of writing about – describing – a naturally occurring woodland that provides the model and inspiration for forest gardening, I realised with utter delight that I was sitting amongst a natural woodland ecosystem that was as good a model for a forest garden as I was ever likely to see, and in fact the first I had ever seen!

Most of the tallest trees were oaks, growing in such a scattered, random fashion, that they did not appear to have been planted or placed by people – they were where nature had put them. The sweet chestnuts were mostly growing separately from the oaks, but some were intermingled. They were generally smaller but a few taller trees showed they could grow to a considerable height if given the room to do so. There were fewer alders, but when I saw them I knew that their significance as natural nitrogen fixers meant that this woodland had the hallmark of an ecosystem that was able to generate its own fertility. I had only previously seen alders in the UK growing in marshy or damp situations often close to rivers, and this woodland was neither wet nor marshy.

At the edge of the woodland there were ferns and brambles twining through each other and small seedling trees (mostly chestnut). From this edge to the cut grass areas designated as camping pitches the ground was clothed in a mixture of wild plants including St John's

Les Bois de St Hilaire, France

wort, dandelions, clove root, nettles, docks, violets, ivy, goose-grass (cleavers), grasses and some other plants I was not familiar with. I am sure their growth is kept in check by the campsite owners but imagine that the varieties are all naturally occurring in that place, as they are commonly occurring wild plants.

Earlier that same morning I had watched a baby rabbit grazing and all day I had been enchanted by the unending birdsong. Bats had flown around the night before and there was a constant procession of bees, butterflies and other insects visiting the flowers.

France was experiencing unusually hot conditions for the time of year and it was arid – there had been a drought for months. I had seen a dried up river bed in a village a few days before. For an hour or so drive both north and south of this point there lay vast expanses of prairie like grain fields with their golden crops on the verge of being harvested. Driving through this countryside the day before had felt a bit like passing through a desert. A grain processing plant with its own railway line lay about half a mile down the road, providing further evidence of the concentration of agriculture on a single crop.

And yet here, in a very quiet corner, undisturbed for (at least) decades, lay this isolated yet thriving little woodland complete with its own range of wild plants and animals. This small, natural woodland was fertile, healthy, diverse and thriving despite being just a fragment in a vast landscape of virtual monoculture (apart from the occasional hedgerow and copse) and in a difficult period of hot and very dry weather. Being there in the wood on that hot summer afternoon it felt alive, happy, co-operative, vital, energising and relaxing all at the same time.

a forest garden ecosystem

This then is the model upon which forest gardening is based. It demonstrates the essential components that form the basis of its ability to function systemically and interact with the natural world.

Forest gardens are structured in descending layers from tall canopy trees to medium-height trees to the shrub and herbaceous plant layers, below which is a ground cover layer and root layer. Climbing plants intermingle between the layers and add further structural interconnections. This structure means that the trees and plants can make the most of the available sunlight and, via photosynthesis, transform it into energy for growth.

Besides the edible trees, bushes and vegetables many more trees and plants are included to perform the necessary functions that enable an ecosystem to form and develop, such as fixing nitrogen, feeding bees and other insects, enriching and enlivening the soil, providing habitat for birds, mammals, and insects, accumulating biomass and storing nutrients. In ecological terms the collective term for the components of an ecosystem is an ecological *guild*. In forest gardening such a collection of multifunctional plants and trees is also called a *polyculture.* I have always been particularly attracted to this description and, as you will find out as you read on, I find it a very apt term for much that occurs within a forest garden.

Another vital aspect of a forest garden is that it is largely perennial. Many trees, bushes and shrubs will live for decades and in a suitably large forest garden some large trees may live for centuries. Alongside these, most of the herbaceous plants are also perennial and will live for a number of years. The longevity of the trees and plants also means a lack of disturbance and the opportunity for the ecosystem to form complex interdependencies between many diverse plants and animals.

These defining elements of a naturally occurring woodland – a layered structure, biodiverse and multifunctional plants, lack of disturbance and perenniality – are also the keys that enable and support the processes of nature in a forest garden and allow it to become healthy, fertile and abundant. Although a forest garden is modelled on natural systems and depends on its interactions with the natural world, it is a human contrivance and not a natural environment. Because of this it is dependent on both the forest gardener and the natural world for its healthy growth and development over time.

It is now apparent how the French woodland I encountered that summer is such a good example of a template for the forest garden 'model'. The layering of the trees means that they are capturing a good deal of the total available sunlight as it strikes the leaves at different heights in the canopy. The trees also provide shade and deposit a layer of mulch across the ground with their annual leaf fall. And below ground they are activating the soil, associating with fungal mycorrhizae, root bonding with other trees. The alder trees do all the above and also fix nitrogen to enrich the soil. Young trees, brambles and ferns comprise the bulk of the lower layer and the mixed herbaceous plants provide a ground cover layer whilst the ivy, honeysuckle and goose-grass climb between these layers. These small to medium plants are also accumulating biomass to eventually feed the soil organisms when they rot down each winter, as well as providing habitat and food for all sorts of insects and possibly small animals too.

In this woodland, as well as the visible and audible animals I had noted, there would have been many other creatures – either hidden in the undergrowth (spiders, beetles, etc.), subterranean (worms, moles) or microscopic organisms, each of them living out their own lives whilst at the same time performing a vital role in the larger system and thereby linking each component organism to every other one. As they inhabit or visit the biodiverse, layered, undisturbed and perennial landscape which has been created for them, it is their presence that makes the whole thing work.

Every plant and animal and fungus both takes from its environment and contributes to it. Everything needs food of some description and produces wastes of some description. Everything dies one day and then donates its body to the ground or the air or the sea where it will be devoured by some other creature. Nothing takes place in isolation. One creature's waste is another creature's food and so it is that nature arranges itself into tightly bound, mutually supportive, interacting systems. All participants give and they take as well, but overall a coherent and cohesive 'structure' is maintained.

The self-sufficiency of a natural ecosystem is crucial to understanding how and why a forest gardener does not need to maintain control. This will be a recurring theme throughout this book that I want to emphasise here at the outset. Allowing nature to create and then augment an ecosystem means that many of the normal gardening tasks are no longer necessary. There are fewer problems with weeds, disease or with 'pests'. A forest gardener is therefore freed from a good deal of labour and can spend more time with the garden, getting to know what is going on and learning how to support nature's work in this place in a much more gentle and appropriate way than they would have thought possible.

To us it is completely and unquestionably normal to make human-centred decisions and top down impositions on the living world, decisions by which we can cause much harm to the earth and all living beings. However, once we see the vital interconnectedness of all living things, we can see ourselves as equal participants in the dance of life and act accordingly.

gardens of delight

I call my forest garden 'the garden of equal delights'. First of all it was simply the garden of delights and I added equal later on – just why will become clear. Hopefully the name garden of delights is self-explanatory – because I find so many delightful things in it and am constantly delighted by it. It is a place to harvest tasty, nutritious, healthy food, a place of great diversity where many creatures now find both food and a home. It is a place of tranquillity, beauty and love. It is edible and a place to live in and to learn from. It was the beauty and joy of it all that brought to mind 'the garden of delights' one day whilst I was roaming around enjoying myself. I had another forest garden before this one, which did not have a name but was equally delightful.

my first garden of delights

What was it that whispered to me that summer afternoon when I first idly wondered if it might be possible to have a garden filled with perennial plants that were also edible – in other words a garden that just grew food year after year with little outside input? Where did that idea drop from? Why did it crystallise in my consciousness? Whatever was that compulsion I felt to find out more and to follow wherever it led? I can't say. I really don't know. However that one moment's questioning thought led me to my first introduction to the concept of forest gardening and I have never looked back. The vision of a beautiful, abundant, edible garden had been born in my heart and I put myself in service of that vision, seeking to create opportunities to enact the vision and to bring it to fruition. From that day onwards I have been inseparably entwined with it.

I wanted my own forest garden to be filled with as many perennial vegetables as possible. I was initially hesitant about starting out on something so new and uncertain because my partner and I had never planned to stay in that home forever; we did not know how long we would be there or if there was time to try out an ambitious project.

The other difficulty was one of scale. Our garden in suburban Telford was just not big enough to accommodate large trees and I was very uncertain about attempting a small-scale forest garden as the only examples I had read about at that time were much larger. However I was so enthused by what I had read about forest gardening that I had become virtually obsessed with the idea of creating my own forest garden. I certainly started out more in hope than expectation, with no certainty that any of the questions I was testing out would bring the results I fervently hoped for. But I decided to have a go anyway with what I had got, in the time that I had, rather than wasting time and wishing for things I did not have and never would.

I took the promise that forest gardening is a low maintenance route to edible abundance at face value, and was very clear from the outset that this was going to be about finding out what was possible for this small patch of land to grow in a natural, unforced way. I was making a new covenant with the garden to dispense with coaxing, controlling or coercing things to grow, I just wanted them to be able to grow if they were suited to being there. I wanted to find out about and obtain as many perennial vegetables as possible and try growing them. I wanted to have as much food as possible growing all year round and to create a functioning ecosystem that would generate its own health and fertility. I was certainly dubious about relying totally on nature to manage the level of slugs and other creatures that might vie with me for the harvests, but was determined to try it out in order to have an ultra-low maintenance garden.

The house and garden were on land that had once been part of an orchard belonging to an old manor house, hence the lovely gnarled old greengage tree we had. The garden had lovely loamy soil from the outset but even this improved and became like dark, sifted, sweet smelling flour as the forest garden matured. The house had been there for nearly fifty years, so the existing garden was well established. It was very pleasant in a conventional way with small and medium-sized trees, shrubs and lawn. There were the usual bulbs in spring and flowering plants in summer. One unusual feature for a town garden was a small stream running along the frontage creating a woodland feel.

To create a forest garden I knew I could make use of the shady conditions provided by the existing trees – willow, rowan, holly, hazel and greengage – and I could plant an understorey layer of fruits and hopefully perennial vegetables. To begin with I was very uncertain about the existence and availability of sufficient suitable perennial vegetables that I would enjoy eating, but fervently hoped I would be able to find enough to make the garden a success. The literature of the time did not have much to say about suitable edible plants that appealed to me and many that they did include were more like unusual herbs such as salad burnet which I didn't find inspiring. It seemed like a very tall order at the time and it was more in hope than expectation that I started out. Even with hindsight I still think it was a big challenge.

Concentrating on the lower layers of a forest garden had an additional benefit because it is these lower, understorey layers – the shrubs, bushes and herbaceous plants – that bring the greatest nutrient recycling into play in a forest garden.

Given my history as a gardener, it was a radical change of direction and approach to decide that I wanted to experiment with growing unusual, hard to find, perennial vegetables. In thirty years I had only ever raised a few seedlings before, and now I was planning to grow potentially dozens of new plants – that was if they even existed and I could obtain them! I was also determined to weave these new plants together into functioning polycultures.

As we have seen, a polyculture is another term for an ecological guild or for a collection of plants that bring together a range of functions to facilitate and maintain a viable ecosystem. Some plants keep pests at bay, others pull minerals from the subsoil or fix nitrogen from the air, keep the ground covered or feed bees and other insects. I therefore needed to learn about and grow all these other plants too.

At the time, even finding information about perennial vegetables was hard – thankfully things have changed a lot in a short time – but with persistence I was able to compile lists of edible plants I wanted to try. The next difficulty was acquiring the seeds, plants, bulbs and tubers (again this is also much easier now). My very first perennial vegetables were walking stick kale and Welsh onions. I have lost count of how many different perennial vegetables I attempted to raise, but I know it was well over fifty – most of which I started off in pots. Nurturing so many young plants was a big challenge, particularly as at that time there were lots of slugs in the garden. I lost a lot and had many disappointments, but also many joyful successes.

There never was an actual plan for the garden as a whole, it just evolved in fits and starts. I don't particularly like planning and tend to avoid it, but it was because it was a small garden and I was not planting any trees at that time that I could afford not to plan. If I had a larger area that would have been foolish, and when in my next garden I planted fruit trees, I did plan where they would go before placing the order for them. There is a balance to be struck between what should sensibly be determined in advance and what can happen on an *ad hoc* moment by moment basis.

I think everyone should do what suits them and their circumstances best. I began by inter-planting experimental perennial vegetables in a border with shrubs and flowering plants. It was a shady spot by a wall and beside a hazel tree, but it did face south and had some sun in the summer. It wasn't long before that border was filled with a variety of perennial kales and other greens and I extended it by planting into the gravel path in front of the bed.

The following year, as the collection continued to grow, I took up some grass in the front garden on the other side of the wall and planted blackcurrants, gooseberries, sweet cicely, fennel, oca, earth nut pea, more kales, Jerusalem artichokes, wild rocket, wild strawberries, field beans and more. This side of the wall was even shadier as it faced north and was close to an apple tree and a small greengage tree, as well as being somewhat in the shade of our house and the bungalow next door. As I continued to find more perennial vegetables, I needed yet more space and the following year the decking was relocated from the centre to the end of the garden and the remaining lawn removed from the back garden. I made new beds, filling the entire space.

This account may make it sound more straightforward than it felt at the time, but after a number of years I realised with delight that I had done what I set out to do. I did indeed have a good range of reliable perennial vegetables on which to base my garden. I felt that I had learned a lot by this time and wrote about it in my book, *Edible Perennial Gardening,* to encourage other people to try something similar. Since then these once unusual plants have become solid, reliable old friends and I could not imagine the garden without them.

As well as the joy of discovering these wonderful edible plants, I had been thrilled with the way the garden had been transformed into a far more beautiful place than it had ever been before when the sole purpose had been to try to create beauty. Admittedly I hadn't been very good at that kind of gardening and now it turned out that nature was proving herself to be much, much better than me.

the garden of equal delights

Eventually the time came for Pat and me to move on. It was heart rending to say goodbye to my treasured garden, but I was able to take plants, cuttings, tubers, bulbs and seeds with me to our new home in Wales and was excited by the opportunity to plant a second forest garden, this time starting completely from scratch.

We now live high on a hill in the borderlands of Wales and England known as the Marches. Here England and Wales more or less melt into each other and travelling to a nearby village takes us across the national boundary twice! It is a very quiet rural area, full of history which lives on today in the Celtic culture of the Welsh people and the ancient monument of Offa's Dyke, which once divided the two countries and passes within half a mile of our home. At 1,000 feet above sea level there are marvellous views across two valleys to the south and the west, and it also has the benefit of exposure to the prevailing wet westerly winds! Because of the elevation the temperature is generally 2°C cooler than in the valley below.

In contrast to the beautiful soil I had inherited in Telford, the soil in this garden is much more of a challenge. The hill we sit atop is comprised of a shaley rock covered with a thin layer of clay. On the

My first forest garden in Telford

Offa's Dyke footpath you can see trees that have fallen because their roots did not get far into the rocky substrate. Both clay and rock lurk at or just below ground level in the garden making it very hard and uninviting for plants and seeds.

The garden is bordered by two hedges – a mixed hedge along the northern roadside edge and a leylandii hedge on the southern boundary. Initially most of the garden was laid to lawn with a few small shrubs planted into landscape fabric and mulched with slate chippings. A driveway to the adjacent properties runs through the garden, cutting it into two halves. My intention for this garden was the same as before – to plant a small-scale forest garden concentrating on the lower layers. I planned to keep things small again partly because of the size of the garden and also because of the wonderful views that were a big part of choosing to live here in the first place. At the time of writing the garden is nearly seven years old - quite young really – it will continue to mature and to be extended further across the lawn for years to come.

Despite a more challenging location and climate than many parts of the UK, the garden has proven to be resilient and has withstood excessive rain, snow, wind and freezing temperatures with little apparent difficulty. However, the heatwave and drought experienced in 2018 were more of a challenge. This was when I noticed a number of aphid infestations for the first time ever. Also some plants grew less that summer and there was less fruit later in the year than I anticipated – but overall it has stood the test of this harsh time well.

I soon realised that I wanted to grow edible plants in all parts of the garden and over the years as I have made new beds, different environments and more possibilities have opened up. At present there are the following beds all packed with both edible and floral plants:

* A mixed edible hedge
* Deep polyculture fruit, flower and vegetable beds
* The 'long border'
* The 'triangle bed'
* The narrow edges around the three shaded sides of the house

In chapter 5, I will explain more about the importance of soil quality, but for now I will just point out that, in a forest garden, living soil is of fundamental importance. The polyculture beds have been prepared in two different ways using methods I made up as I went along.

the first polyculture bed

The first polyculture bed in this garden was constructed on top of the lawn alongside the house. The soil beneath the lawn was a thin smear of very hard clay interspersed with, and underlain by, rocks. I could not have got a spade into it even if I had wanted to. Because I don't bring any materials in from outside and I don't dig, I needed to create a bed to grow my early transplanted perennial vegetables from what was at hand. I gathered as many organic materials as I could from the garden to make something to plant in to. There was ivy from the mixed hedge (including its roots) and what I could pull out from beneath the hedge by way of humus-rich materials. The latter was the end product of hedge cuttings that had fallen to the ground and composted down over the previous years before I lived there. I sprinkled these unlikely materials on the ground and covered them in due course with lawn cuttings and hedge trimmings as they became available.

Much of the bed that first year was no more than these basic materials. The bed was edged with stones and with a woven stick edge using hazel stems from the hedge. Piling organic material onto the lawn means that this was effectively a raised bed, but it is quite different from the horticultural style raised bed with straight wooden edges and filled with purchased compost or topsoil.

Into this odd mixture I planted root crops brought from my first garden – Jerusalem artichoke, yacon, oca, mashua, plus herbs, beans, peas and other assorted plants. It made a surprisingly green and luxuriant garden although not surprisingly most of the growth was top growth and the actual harvest of roots was not great. By the following year this organic material had rotted down into a very nice

Constructing the first polyculture bed in May
The first polyculture bed in September

fertile humusy mixture and would have continued to improve. However we had plans for a new conservatory just where this bed was. I moved all the newly created soil and plants across to the other side of the garden to start again!

subsequent polyculture beds

The long border and the triangle bed near the house were formed when I removed the turf, and planted directly into the soil that was exposed. In these beds the work of soil building is proceeding slowly. There was no organic matter to speak of in the beginning and probably no decomposer organisms. To break up the hard and stony soil I introduced lots of plants with tap roots and tubers – perennial vegetables such as Japanese burdock, scorzonera, Jerusalem artichoke, oca, salsify and also allowed wild plants like dandelions and docks, to 'dig' the soil for me.

On the other side of the garden I made four deep beds. They have a base of dead wood taken from the hedge and covered with upturned turf taken from the long border and triangle bed. I planted into this mixture and mulched them with lawn cuttings and other plant material as it became available.

the mixed edible hedge

This originally comprised blackthorn, hawthorn, damson, hazel, elder, holly, sycamore and ash. To this I have added a number of edible climbers including hops, akebia quinata, blackberries and kiwi fruit. There are raspberries, jostaberries, figs, bay, goji berries, gooseberries and red, white and black currants, plus berry bushes for the birds – berberis, cotoneaster, pyracantha. Then there are perennial wild onions, wild strawberries, and an array of wildflowers. Again there was no advance planning, I just put things in as they became available and tried to thicken up the hedge, making it in effect a double layer of the original trees on the inside and the edibles on the outside.

the edge bed

Around the house there is a narrow strip between the boundary hedge and fence, and the house. Into this is planted a mix of all kinds of plants – basically anything that won't fit into any other place but which needs a home.

a different garden

I have said that a forest garden is a different garden because it is based on the model of a natural woodland and because it is a vibrant, healthy, functioning ecosystem. But what does that mean in practice? Why is my garden different? What makes it special?

Over time I have planted a lot of fruit trees and bushes and mixed up perennial vegetables, annual vegetables, herbs, with both cultivated and wildflowers amongst them. The result is that the garden looks different and much more densely vegetated than a 'normal' garden. Some – mainly the fruits – are familiar; others – mainly the vegetables – are not.

*Apple Trwyn Mochyn (foreground), jostaberries (background,
spring flowers and edibles (centreground)*

All the plants have freedom to set seed which means that they
appear in unconventional, but often very lovely, combinations. Some
of the unexpected flowers are actually exquisitely beautiful – parsley
and carrot are two of my favourites.

The sheer number of flowers is another important difference. I have
deliberately concentrated on including plants that bear thousands
and thousands of minute flowers as these have proven to be amazing
for insects. From spring to late summer there is an extravagant
profusion of flowers and as a result there are more flying insects
than I have ever seen anywhere else, visiting the many thousands of
flowers. From the early bumble bee queens emerging in spring to
the honeybees, hoverflies and butterflies of summer, the air is
always buzzing. There are more bees, butterflies and other insects
every year and I am wondering if this is because there is ever more

habitat for them as well as food. I will return to this theme in chapter 10.

This summer many of our visitors have stopped and spent prolonged periods of time studying the garden, watching the bees and butterflies and making comments like 'have you got all the bees in the world here?'

The garden is far from neat and tidy and you could also get the impression that it is crowded, muddled, full of weeds and with heaps of 'stuff' everywhere. Indeed there are piles of mulch in some places which are sometimes plainly visible and at other times hidden beneath plenteous growth.

Going beyond initial appearances there is a rich diversity of species – over two hundred plants, of which more than one hundred are edible. The table below shows the numbers of each type of edible plant, and a full list of everything currently growing in the garden is given in appendix 1.

plant type	number
Fruits	29
Perennial vegetable greens	8
Self-seeding annual greens	2
Perennial root vegetables	9
Self-seeding root vegetables	2
Onions	11
Herbs	20
Conventional vegetables	4
Edimentals[3] (ornamental plants that are also edible)	19
Total	**104**

As the garden has matured it has offered increasing harvests with something to be gathered and eaten all year round. In winter and

[3] This is a word coined by Stephen Barstow. His book *Around the World in 80 Plants* has detailed descriptions of many interesting and attractive edible plants.

spring there are kales, early wild onions and salad greens. The summer brings all sorts of fruits including currants, gooseberries, raspberries, jostaberries, strawberries, plums, cherries, plus peas, beans, garlic and more onions. In autumn the kales start to grow prolifically again and there are apples, pears and root vegetables including oca, Jerusalem artichoke and skirret. There are also herbs for cooking and flowers for cutting from spring to autumn.

I care for this garden just as I cared for the previous one, but now I understand better what I am doing and why it has the effects it does. There is much more explanation to come about this, but for now I will say that I never dig the garden and I only remove wild plants (so-called weeds) when absolutely necessary – which is *not* on sight. I never use any kind of pest control. I only water new plants for a short while to settle them in and others only in extreme conditions – this has so far happened in the summer of 2018 when I watered the newly planted trees through the worst of the summer heat. I used rainwater until it ran out and eventually had to resort to a hosepipe. After a bit some of the fruit bushes that were about to ripen also became distressed through lack of water and I gave them some drinks as well. There is no compost heap in the garden and I never use any fertilisers. Apart from new trees, plants and seeds, nothing is imported into the garden to support it; and apart from produce eaten by us or given away, nothing is exported from it either, and it seems to become more fertile and productive all the time.

Because there is so much that I never do, actual gardening takes up much less time than in a conventional garden – and that is one of the great things about it. I am writing this in early October and I have hardly done anything for months – most of the 'work' in the garden since spring has been picking fruit! Because the plants are virtually all perennial or self-seeding annuals, I don't have to sow seeds, tend tiny plants or remove spent ones. It basically just takes care of itself – which, of course, as an ecosystem it should do.

As time has gone on, I have added other plants to the garden regardless of their edibility and other considerations, just because I like them. So now if I want another rose or penstemon – in they go!

All the intentionally planted plants grow entwined with each other and with plenty of self-introduced wildflowers.

The following chapters will explain in detail how and why doing so little can result in a productive and beautiful garden, and how a forest gardener learns to integrate themselves into the ecosystem. As well as those benefits, I see another, deeper aspect to forest gardening – to me being a forest gardener is a portal to a different way of being human. As a forest gardener I am not in charge or control of this garden, it is a place of co-creation with nature and it is as productive as it is beautiful. I love it; it is my garden of equal delights.

principles of forest gardening

And so we invite you to a lifetime of quiet adventure. Ecological systems at their essence operate on simple principles yet have endlessly fascinating intricacies.

~ Jacke & Toensmeier

After some years of forest gardening and finding my own particular way of interacting with my garden, I asked myself 'how would I describe or explain what I do in the garden to someone else?' and 'how do I decide what I will do and what I will refrain from doing?' Would it translate to any or all other forest gardens?

From the outset, gardening my forest garden was different to all the gardening I had ever done before. I have found new ways to do things in the garden, and at least as important, ways of not doing things too. I make decisions on a day-by-day, moment-by-moment basis, being well aware that these decisions are always subjective and are predicated on the current context, on sensitivity to the garden and on weighing up the appropriateness of any actions. Would it ever be possible to adequately describe something that could, on the face of it, appear quite random?

This was the beginning of an intensive questioning of precisely what I do and why I do it – a questioning that continued to evolve all the time this book was being written. I needed to know what *exactly* I had learned from interacting with my forest garden that I did not know before. I would need to demonstrate what this learning was and precisely how I had acquired it. Furthermore, could I pass on this learning to others, given that my garden is but one particular expression of a forest garden? As my gardening was and is nothing like conventional gardening and has no specified or regular routines or activities, I had unwittingly presented myself with a bigger challenge than I first thought.

The testing ground has been my forest garden in Wales for it was there that these questions first arose. But I can also look back to my time in my first forest garden in Telford and recognise the same patterns of interaction with that garden as well.

I reasoned that if there is coherence in this universe, if everything is in fact related to everything else there must be recognisable patterns to discern, and perhaps from this it would be possible to derive a set of principles. I noticed from my own actions in the garden that, by learning to relate to nature, I had indeed, over time, learned some practical principles which I could see guided my decision-making in the garden and I had some rough and ready sayings I used to guide what I was doing. This was the starting point, but there was still the much larger question of how to elucidate them, pin them down and put them into words.

And so it was that I went into the garden to be with it and to become aware of our mutual relationship. I went to watch the garden and to listen to my own internal voice, my reasoning, to observe my responses to the garden's cues and its responses to my previous involvement, my doing and non-doing. I spent much time thus and much, much, much more time afterwards pondering, examining, delving, sifting and letting be.

Forest gardening is often seen as part of the wider repertoire of permaculture and I considered the principles of permaculture developed by David Holmgren, and listed in and briefly discussed in appendix 2. However I could not find a true fit between these principles and my way of being with the garden. There was some common ground, overlap and agreement in part but there were also gaps and bits that didn't quite fit. So I reasoned I would have to deduce my own principles direct from the garden.

I examined my experience in the past as I recalled decisions made. In the present I watched my thoughts as I went through the process of deciding to take action or not. I endlessly questioned myself and my emerging answers to test them out. I looked for common threads that were derived from the garden and always applicable to it, in all circumstances. Writing this now makes it sound like even more of a challenge – how would I unfold the answers I was looking for?

This has been a long process and an intense one. Eventually the content and derivation of the principles emerged and identified themselves. They are all inter-related and sometimes overlapping. Each principle is a new step on the journey from control to trust. In the process of writing I have gone over and over these, inspected their veracity, looking for ways to explain them that relate to the story of the garden, and my story too, as well as checking for other information that may be necessary to fully understand or explain them. I have listed them below and the remainder of this book explains their derivation, their meaning and their effects.

principles of forest gardening

* Forest gardening is based upon the structure, composition and functioning of a natural woodland including the resultant ecosystem and its emergent properties. In a forest garden biodiversity means health; a living soil and increasing biomass mean increasing fertility, and together health and fertility mean abundance.
* First stop; don't do anything until you need to and, in that prolonged pause, let go
* Everything the forest gardener does takes full account of the whole of the forest garden ecosystem – what has happened, what is happening and what they intend for the future
* Watch and wait
* When you have to do something, only do the minimum
* Plant polyfloral polycultures everywhere
* As far as possible the trees and plants in a forest garden should live for their full life span and reproduce themselves naturally and unaided
* Support nature's transformational magic
* Whether in abundance or not, harvest only enough
* Demonstrate appreciation in meaningful and tangible ways

* Polyculture learning is slow learning
* Welcome the wild

I have also considered the question of whether the size of the forest garden makes any difference and therefore if these insights are applicable to gardens that are larger than mine. My answer to that question is yes, because being principles and not instructions they are always open to the interpretation of the gardener in the context of their garden and at any scale you can pause, watch, wait, plant polyfloral polycultures, support nature's transformational magic and more. In the end everything comes down to having an understanding of the ecological processes occurring in a forest garden, making sure you support them and don't interfere with or interrupt them unnecessarily.

I see these principles as metaphorical seeds, representations of complex realities wrapped in simple statements, as possibilities waiting for experience to unwrap them, as an open door to the path that leads to a freer, more relational, unique-to-you interaction with your garden.

fertility, health and abundance

principle 1

Forest gardening is based upon the structure, composition and functioning of a natural woodland including the resultant ecosystem and its emergent properties. In a forest garden biodiversity means health; a living soil and increasing biomass mean increasing fertility, and together health and fertility mean abundance

I think of this as the foundational principle because it holds within it just about everything needful to know; that is to say that everything in the forest garden and the forest gardener's experience relates directly to this principle. It will become clearer as we progress on this forest garden journey but for now let me begin to unwrap its meaning and some simple, practical applications.

The actions (and non-actions) of the forest gardener are all for the purpose of encouraging a resilient ecosystem, including a healthy soil food web, and there are three very simple things that a forest gardener needs to do:

* Encourage biodiversity by growing as many different perennial plants in the garden as possible.
* Have as much volume of plant material (biomass) growing in the garden as possible.
* When plants or trees die or are cut back, feed everything (i.e. all the biomass) directly back to the garden without composting it first.

The following explanations rely heavily on my understanding and practical interpretation of the work of Dave Jacke and Eric Toensmeier. I have made very good use of their two books, having re-read them repeatedly before starting my first forest garden, and I still frequently refer to them. Natural ecosystems are incredibly complex and I have space (and understanding) for only the most cursory explanation here. However, cursory or not I believe it is sufficient for this purpose. I would recommend anyone who would like a more detailed, fully referenced and evidenced description and explanation of the ecology of a forest garden to refer to Jacke and Toensmeier's work directly.

biodiversity means health

Within a healthy and thriving ecosystem all the animals, plants and fungi are there to interact with each other, which in practice often means eating and/or being eaten. So there is much more going on in the garden than the trees and plants that the conventional gardener tends to focus on. Everything from the smallest soil bacteria to the worms, spiders, beetles, bees, butterflies, mice, birds, squirrels, foxes and hedgehogs, and whatever else lives in the locality and can find food or habitat there, may be drawn into this ever increasing ecosystem. A forest garden is predicated upon all of this life finding a mutually healthy and reasonably stable balance. To that end Jacke and Toensmeier say that diversity:

* Produces more niches for different plants and animals to inhabit
* Reduces competition
* Increases productivity and yield
* Generates functional interconnection
* Generates stability and resilience
* Reduces herbivory
* Creates beauty

The more plant species and varieties within the forest garden the greater the number of animals of all kinds that can visit or live in the garden and this means that more of the niches or roles in the cyclical processes of life are filled. Fewer gaps means more stability, greater resilience and health. For example, if aphids arrive in my garden in spring when the plants are growing ultra-fast this is not a problem. They are not pests, they are part of the whole and because the garden also houses or hosts insects that will devour these aphids, then all will be well. The aphids are actually food; they are low, low down the food chain, but they are food nonetheless that fuels slightly larger creatures who then feed others and so on. No aphids ultimately means less food for everyone. The same goes for slugs, caterpillars, rabbits or anything that might be thought of as a pest. There is more on this topic in chapter 12.

One very simple action that stems from valuing biodiversity is to welcome wild plants into the garden. Over time I have seen many benefits to this, especially the very visible benefit of their attractiveness to pollinating insects – it seems to me that bees, butterflies, flies and all sorts of insects much prefer wildflowers to conventional garden plants, including those labelled in nurseries as good bee plants. This does not mean that no wild plant will ever be removed, but that it is never blind, unthinking dogma that informs decision making. As the forest gardener becomes increasingly integrated with the garden they are able to make decisions for the benefit of the whole garden. The watching and waiting (which I will describe in much more detail later) are the fuel and focus for this decision-making.

living soil

Healthy soil is very much alive and a healthy soil food web provides many benefits including:

* Increased nutrient retention, cycling and availability to plants
* Improved crop quality
* Pest and disease suppression
* Improved soil structure, drainage, aeration, water holding, habitat
* Production of plant growth factors
* Decomposition of toxic chemicals and pollutants
* A cleaner environment

As I noted in *Edible Perennial Gardening*, "It is the concept of a web of life in the soil which has stuck firmly in my mind and imagination and has helped me to understand how to help the soil become healthy and fertile. It has become a very important consideration that guides everything I do (and don't do) in the garden."

A lifeless soil – i.e. one from which all living plants have been removed – comprises only mineral particles, water and air. Nutrients can only be acquired very, very slowly from bedrock, from mineral particles or from the atmosphere. When it rains many of the available nutrients are leached down to the subsoil and lost, and there is no food for any soil organisms.

Imagine an empty vegetable patch or allotment in winter that has had some undecomposed or partially decomposed organic matter added to it. This will stimulate some activity of what is called the 'dead food web' by feeding the organisms that live on dead organic matter. This will increase the water-holding capacity of the soil and benefit its structure. But once the organic matter is all decomposed and the decomposer organisms have completed their job, they will die, unless more dead organic material becomes available. And all the while winter rains will leach nutrients downwards, out of reach of next year's plants. This is a vulnerable soil, and it is dependent on the gardener continuing to add fertiliser of some kind to it.

It is plants that introduce and maintain life and thereby make a world of difference.

* Plants provide the majority of the organic matter in the system through litter fall and root die back
* Plant roots extract nutrients from soil water, preventing leaching
* Plants use water for transpiration which also prevents leaching
* Plants radically increase the diversity and abundance of soil organisms in the root zone (5-10 times more fungi and 10-50 times more bacteria). They do this by feeding microbes energy-rich root secretions (exudates). The expanding microbial populations are another store of soil nutrients
* Perennial plants absorb nutrients in autumn to use the following year

Because they are permanent the trees, bushes, shrubs and herbaceous perennials in a forest garden are the vital basis for a healthy living food soil web.

carbon sequestration

Another very significant aspect of a healthy soil is its ability to store, or sequester, carbon. Through photosynthesis plants use sunlight to convert atmospheric carbon dioxide and water to carbohydrates such as glucose, starches and cellulose. On average 50% of a plant's dry weight is carbon; in soils that are not subjected to disturbances (such as digging), when part, or all, of the plant dies back and falls to the ground, one third of this carbon is stored for the long term within the soil's organic matter. A plant's roots equate to between 25 and 40% of its top-growth; each year some of these die back and also contribute to the long term stores of organic matter.

In addition it is estimated that between 10 and 40% of all photo-synthesised carbon passes through the roots as sugary exudates within an hour. In healthy soils a variety of bio-geo-chemical processes aggregate these sugars with inorganic particles adding to the reservoir of carbon sequestered for the long term.

There is currently a great deal of interest in the carbon sequestration potential of different agroforestry practices and the evidence to date suggests that if used on a large enough scale these practices – which include forest gardening – could play a significant role in removing carbon from the atmosphere.

It is important to note that compacted soils are not conducive to microbial activity and outside of the root zone many organisms are dormant. But if shredding and chewing invertebrates such as worms, beetles, grubs, larvae, centipedes and the like are present, they provide the perfect conditions for a microbial population explosion. Furthermore, the beneficial bacteria in the soil are adversely affected by disturbance, lack of oxygen, excessive wetness and high nitrate or chemical levels, whereas pathogenic bacteria are more able to tolerate such conditions and are therefore positively selected for by traditional gardening methods.

One other key component of a living soil is a network of mycorrhizal fungi which grow into the roots of host trees and plants and exchange nutrients for sugars. In undisturbed soils they can spread for miles, effectively linking all the plants and trees together and supporting them by:

* Gathering water and nutrients
* Extending the life of plant roots
* Protecting plant roots from predators, pathogens, salt and toxic heavy metals
* Aggregating soil particles
* Weathering minerals and organic matter
* Mediating plant-to-plant interactions
* Evolving speedily to help cope with change

With perennial plants, mycorrhizal fungi and soil micro-organisms linked together by mutually beneficial interactions, the living soil in a forest garden retains and recycles the available nutrients, conserves water and protects against pathogens and pollutants.

increasing biomass means increasing fertility

The more biomass there is in a forest garden, the greater the potential fertility. Every plant that lives in a natural ecosystem will die and decompose where it once stood and the same needs to be largely true of a forest garden. This is why I feed everything that has grown in the garden directly back to it. I want as much growth (biomass) as possible because when it is fed directly back to the soil it increases the organic matter, thereby creating and sustaining a self-perpetuating beneficial cycle. How this works in practice is explored in detail in chapter 8.

abundance is an emergent property

A full understanding of how any actual ecosystem functions is beyond a book like this. However just the absolute basics that I have explained in this chapter show the potential for a self-enhancing cycle of benefits. More biodiversity creates the conditions for yet more life in the garden, helps to feed all of life and keeps the garden healthy. More biomass (some of which will come from the additional biodiversity) feeds the soil and boosts growth, which in turn generates yet more biomass.

Where there is fertility and health there will also be abundance; these are the emergent properties of the ecosystem created in a forest garden. Having a token ecosystem is not enough. A forest garden needs to be *teeming and seething with life*. Thus the actual work of a forest gardener is primarily putting together and then fostering a network of relationships between plants and other life forms and between plants and soil. In the following chapters, I will explore what this relationship between forest gardener and forest garden comprises and more about how it works in practice.

part 2

is gardened differently

stop, don't do anything until you need to

principle 2

First stop; don't do anything until you need to and, in that prolonged pause, let go

> "I was aiming at a pleasant, natural way of farming which results in making the work easier instead of harder. 'How about not doing this? How about not doing that?' – that was my way of thinking. When you get right down to it there are few agricultural practices which are really necessary."
>
> ~ Masanobu Fukuoka

The forest garden is planted, everything is in place – what is the first thing the forest gardener needs to do? It is to *stop*!

Go and make a cup of tea or meet up with friends for coffee. Go out for the day. Go on holiday. Read a book, watch a film, visit an elderly neighbour. Go and do nothing or do something, but whatever you do leave the garden alone. This is important. You have done your bit for now. It is time for the garden to start to do its own thing in its own way. The garden needs time and space – freedom from human interference. So, off you go – and do something else for a bit.

in the pause, or the story of letting go

Starting out by stopping may sound like the strangest bit of gardening advice you have ever heard. However it is not just important, it is vital. It is the heart of the matter. To be a forest gardener is to embrace a freedom unknown to horticulture. First in theory, and then in practice. It means giving freedom away – passing it on, freely, directly, happily, willingly, with trust and in time with love, to the forest garden. To do this the gardener stops what they previously knew as gardening.

I learned this initially from Masanobu Fukuoka and (although I have a garden and not a farm) the quote above is the simplest and most profound and valuable piece of advice that I have had from anywhere. *This advice is absolutely fundamental to everything I have learned from and about my garden from that day forward.* I feel a huge debt of gratitude to Fukuoka for his book *One Straw Revolution* and his insightful, respectful and wise ways of growing food.

The principle of non-action is derived entirely from my experience of following this gentle advice which has been in my mind, my heart and my practice continually. It is deceptive in its simplicity and an outright confrontation to us humans who love to do, to be busy, to implement and by all these means to control. Of course, the obvious questions that arise as a result are:

* How will I know when the time for waiting is over and something is to be done?
* When that time comes what will I then do?

But before rushing on to more about taking action, let's first of all have a look at what does not happen during this prolonged pause.

in the pause

The initial injunction to stop is in effect introducing a prolonged pause into the forest gardener's life. This is a powerful principle, which I took on experimentally in my initial eagerness to find out how little I could get away with doing. But I learned much more than simply finding ways to avoid work: I learned that the garden was much better able to become the garden I was hoping for if I let nature get on with what it does day in and day out. And through this prolonged pausing I learned just about everything I now know about practical forest gardening. It is the heart of being a forest gardener because it is the only true way of ceasing to control. At the beginning of this prolonged pause the forest gardener is in the dark – like a seed waiting to grow, waiting for new sensitivities to awaken and pull it in a different direction.

the story of letting go

Once control is relinquished the doorway is open to an entirely new way of being in and with the garden. Pausing, waiting, stopping – whatever you call not doing – all open up a space firstly for other things to happen and secondly to learn from those happenings. They are all in fact different dimensions of one state of being. That is, the state of 'being with' the garden and everything growing in it, everything living in it and everything happening in it. It is perhaps the first step on the way to polyculture mind.

In this pause the forest gardener has received freedom; now is the time to pass that freedom on to the garden. This means that letting go is equally part of the pause, part of waiting, watching, noticing, allowing things to (just) be and crucially also allowing yourself the same luxury. Pausing and letting go are emphatically not complacency and certainly not laziness. This is about never-ending learning and evolving, even (or particularly) when it is happening subconsciously.

This is a testing ground for our intention to act on the understanding of everything that we have learned to this point. In other words that this is a co-creative venture with the natural world and requires only that we relax and have the integrity to let nature make its moves without vetoing them, without placing sanctions on what it does and without arbitrary, ill-considered and vain judgements. This will be difficult, but for now the new forest gardener can take refuge in their knowledge of ecosystems, biodiversity, soil fertility and the multiple abilities of plants. This knowledge is at least a buffer against the uncertainty and inevitable anxiety engendered by not being in control.

freedom from control and activity

The virtually inevitable result of imagining doing nothing in any garden is to foresee chaos, an overgrown jungle or something similar. That is what all our conditioning leads us to expect. However, in a natural ecosystem, water is regulated, soil is created and enriched, fertility is generated and distributed, new plants and trees germinate, wild plants flourish and pests and disease are usually kept in balance. In a horticultural garden, the gardener waters the garden, digs and tends the soil, makes compost and applies fertiliser. I see these traditional horticultural activities as limiting of life and variety, and replacing them with natural processes helps the garden move towards greater diversity, health and vigour. A forest garden therefore renders these conventional tasks obsolete and the forest gardener can relinquish the responsibility for hydration, fertility and soil building. The forest gardener is not redundant – they still have a part to play in respect of these vital processes, but a part that will support nature and not work contrary to it.

For most gardeners there are two sorts of plants – those they want and those they don't. The latter are usually wild plants and usually called weeds. The main aim of horticultural gardening is to nurture the plants the gardener wants and to uproot or otherwise destroy those that are not wanted. The thinking behind this is that weeding is essential, otherwise the weeds will take over, the garden will become wild or overgrown, there will be no crop or no flowers and it will be a disaster. Weeds then are identified as 'other' – they are not wanted, they have no use. This is the garden equivalent of hatred, prejudice, bigotry and discrimination.

In a conventional garden, weeding is the epitome of control. It is a reflex action, conditioned into us from our earliest days. Some plants (those we have chosen) are good, some plants (those we have not chosen, but which have actually chosen us) are bad. They *must go* and that is all there is to it – an unthinking reflex. Of course, horticulture cannot work without this level of control, but forest gardens will not and cannot work with it.

Within the logic and methods of horticulture these attitudes are entirely reasonable and logical. But the forest gardener is operating from a different paradigm and is endeavouring to support an ecosystem. In this ecosystem everything has a function and is an integral part of a single complex unity. The forest gardener is learning not to just turn a blind eye to the wild plants (the weeds), but is beginning to appreciate their value as living beings contributing to the forest garden and having their own purpose and place within this world. This does not mean that every wild plant that arrives in the forest garden should stay indefinitely, but it definitely does mean that they should not automatically be removed without a second thought. In time the forest gardener will recognise the wild plant as a gift, an opportunity, a delight, as beautiful and as an intrinsic part of this place.

Choosing to do less is crucial because it allows complexity to evolve. The forest gardener and forest garden evolve together, so loosen up, lighten up, give your garden some space, some freedom, some independence, some respect, some credit.

non-activities for letting go

Just in case this is making you really uneasy, here are some things to get on with not doing at this point!

* Not watering
* Not composting
* Not digging
* Not 'weeding'
* Not controlling pests
* Not fertilising
* Not using a green bin
* Not dead-heading
* Not clearing to bare soil

The following table lists the standard jobs necessary for maintaining a conventional garden. Some of these I see as potentially or actually harmful tasks of control which replace the natural functioning of an ecosystem and can damage it. The others I think of as techniques, none of which are harmful, and some of which are still useful and even necessary for the forest gardener.

Tasks of control	Reasons
Pest control including chemicals, biological control, organics, companion planting, fruit cages, netting, etc.	Some of these means are damaging and some are benign, but none are necessary in a forest garden because pests are controlled by the operation of the ecosystem.
Clearing the land back to bare soil	This never happens in nature, unless as a result of a natural disaster. It permits a loss of soil and of nutrients and is damaging.
Dead-heading of flowers	Self-seeding is encouraged and necessary in a natural ecosystem or a forest garden, so flowers are not routinely dead-headed.
Weeding	This is not a routine task in a forest garden, but some self-sown wild plants are removed as required.
Removing plants when they have finished flowering or their edible parts have been harvested	This is not a routine task but may still be required in a forest garden.
Digging the garden	This damages the soil structure and kills its microbiotic life and is not needed in a forest garden, apart from digging planting holes and harvesting root vegetables.

Techniques	Notes
Raised beds	Deep soil is good and to be encouraged but it is not necessary to construct uniformly shaped raised beds with timber edges as these act as barriers to life interconnecting across the garden and to my mind are a visual impediment as well. The benefits of raised beds are generated within the garden as living soil accumulates.
Use of green bin or local recycling facility	This is not necessary. The ecosystem will collect and dispose of all spare or waste plant material. Not to use this biomass within the garden is wasteful and actually depletes the ecosystem which is then feeding its nourishment to far-flung places and squandering energy in the process.
Making compost	This is not necessary as natural processes operate at ground level and decompose plant material in situ where it grew.
Mulching	This happens in a forest garden, but not in the same way as a conventional garden. More details in chapter 8.
Regular watering or irrigation	New trees and plants need to be watered in to establish them. Thereafter watering is only necessary very occasionally in extreme conditions. Generally the soil and the ecosystem manage the drainage and distribution of water.
Cutting back or pruning plants	This is necessary for cultivated fruit trees and bushes and will be needed for other shrubs and plants in a forest garden at times.
Raising seedlings	This is likely to be necessary at first and may always be needed depending on the aims for the forest garden.
Creating new plants by vegetative propagation	As above.

responsibility relinquished[4]

The fundamental functions planned for in a forest garden are but the bare bones (or maybe the bare branches) upon which nature can hang ever-greater complexity brought into the garden from beyond its boundary. Whilst the forest gardener can have a basic grasp of what is needed, what we are actually aiming to replicate is complex far beyond our understanding. And, precisely because of this complexity, much of it can be left directly to nature. The forest gardener cannot manage this alone; we must never think we can.

Nevertheless, there is an active and essential role for the forest gardener. A forest garden is, to my mind, a garden that potentially achieves more than nature would do if left alone in this place. It will almost certainly have a greater diversity of species than would arrive naturally and it may generate more growth and therefore more biomass. Additional biodiversity and biomass both mean that more complexity will be invited in to find a home in the garden. So I think of a forest garden not as a (semi) natural ecosystem but as an augmented ecosystem and a place for the gardener to help and support nature in gathering up its disparate and lost threads that have been scattered far and wide.

As a result, the forest gardener is released from the responsibility that they may be tempted to feel, of having to ensure that the forest garden works. There is no regular watering, no weeding, no pest control, no compost making and other gardening tasks that remain are required far less often than before. So many of the regular tasks of gardening are now undertaken by nature and have become superfluous. The forest gardener is restored to their rightful niche in the garden where they fit in unobtrusively, but nevertheless effectively. Being freed from a lot of routine tasks gifts the gardener much more time.

---

[4] The early drafts of this chapter were about constraints and keeping within particular parameters. Such is the measure of the modern mind's alliance with doing and controlling that it took me nearly a year to realise that, because forest gardening is predicated on what nature does far more than upon what people do, what I was really writing about was freedom.

control and complexity

Conventional gardening is about control and to exercise control is to attempt to create certainty and to create an artificial simplicity. In contrast to the artificial simplicity we are used to and understand, forest gardening asks us to co-operate with ecosystems and polycultures that are intrinsically complex. There is no certainty in forest gardening and we need to understand complexity as our friend in this natural system; it is a complexity that can be trusted to work without any particular input from the gardener.

This is about learning patience, remaking and remodelling our expectations. By pausing and offering time and attention you are offering yourself, and that is *all* anyone actually has to offer. What is more, this is unconditional offering and there is no proxy or substitute for it. This is the only way to learn and to bond in this story of unravelling self-interest.

the twin story of waiting and watching

principle 3

Everything the forest gardener does takes full account of the whole of the forest garden ecosystem – what has happened, what is happening and what they intend for the future

A more concise way of saying this would be to say that the forest gardener gardens with the forest, and that this provides the context for *everything* that they do from this point on. The next two principles follow as a direct consequence of this one and help to unwrap and explain it. Because the gardener is aiming to become an integral part of the forming ecosystem they dedicate themselves to learning its ways. They do this by watching and waiting and then by using their growing understanding to interact with the garden, responding to the activity of nature within the garden and taking the initiative to make desired or necessary changes.

I will return to this later in chapter 9.

principle 4

Watch and wait

Watching and waiting is not primarily about what is seen – hence it is not observation. It is not watching to learn, rather it is learning to watch - and thereby ultimately to learn. Watching and waiting is also about the internal changes effected in the forest gardener, unbidden and probably unnoticed at first. Changes that will reconfigure us in nature's mould, and about which there is much more to say later on.

watching

Watching is the only way to know what is happening and thereby to come to some understanding, and understanding is essential to making decisions. So firstly there is *how you watch*, secondly there is *what you watch* and thirdly there is *some understanding of what you have seen.*

watching with polyculture eyes

Watching a forest garden or a polyculture is not like watching a conventional vegetable patch or garden: we do not focus on looking for specific things like weeds between the crops, or potential problems, or even the amount of produce we may eventually get. The forest garden is a unity, but it is a complex unity. Every individual thing we see is looked at in the context of how the polyculture as a whole is faring. So we watch in order to soak everything up. We watch with polyculture eyes.

Polyculture eyes see everything – just as it is – for the sake of seeing alone. No other purpose or agenda directs their gaze this way or that. Because they have no mandate other than to watch, they are patient, becoming utterly absorbed in, and fascinated by, the smallest of changes, witnessing its growth and change, letting it be what it is.

Have you watched your garden as winter closes and spring unfolds and unfurls? Eagerly watched for the earliest, tiniest indications of life returning and pushing green leaves from the soil and from bare brown twigs? Have you ever watched a plant closely enough to know the time it takes for its first leaf to unfurl and what shape that leaf makes? How it arises from a barely visible point and swells to its full size? Have you seen the same leaf you watched being born, dying? Have you seen it wither and change colour and fall to the ground? And then watched it dissolve and disappear?

Have you watched a flower open its petals one by one? Have you seen insects arrive and depart and have you seen the same petals turning brown and dropping away? Have you watched the seed head it leaves behind swell and ripen, dry out and split open to spill or eject is valuable contents? To shake, scatter, blow or pop them towards a fresh start? Have you enjoyed the sight of a tiny fruit as it swells to maturity?

This kind of watching is about letting nature in. It is watching in a 'being with' way much more than an 'observing' way. To watch like this, seeing everything all year round – this is the watching of polyculture eyes. Watching with polyculture eyes requires us to immerse ourselves in the garden. This is a particular quality of seeing, not a tick list of things seen and duly noted.

There is an equality in the forest garden that does not exist in other gardens (or possibly in other places, full stop); equality between the beings. All are part of the web of life that both comprises and sustains this garden. Polyculture eyes do not see individual plants in isolation, but as integral to the whole garden. They are actively looking for and watching all members of the ecosystem. They are looking for the purpose of the garden to be made manifest and for their own vision coming into being.

Polyculture eyes feed into the other senses and into intuition. They are part of revaluing – they do not see weeds or pests but new plants and new animals. All plants and all animals of whatever size and reputation are dependent upon one another and all are equally necessary in the forest garden. Therefore polyculture eyes see the evolving forest garden from many perspectives: they look through nature's eyes to take on the perspective of the worm, the bird or the bee, the mole, the mouse and the vole. They watch all the animals that turn up, see where they go, what they eat, where they rest, nest or sleep.

These eyes store all this up, and much more besides. They know this garden, in every season and in every aspect. And as the polyculture eyes see more all the time, polyculture mind becomes more acutely aware of the minutiae of forest garden life. Ever more discerning and increasingly well-informed, polyculture mind hones the gardener's perceptions, takes everything in and mulls it over. I *began to feel freer in the very early days as I* watched the garden unfold into previously undreamt of possibilities. Watching your garden in this way and for extended periods without intervening will teach you to your core that you have entered into a deep and patient partnership with it.

what you watch

What do you see in the pause when you first watch your forest garden? In the beginning I had no idea that polyculture eyes were part of the forest gardener's skills and I wasn't paying attention to my own watching. Nevertheless I watched almost ferociously from the outset. I watched for every sign of growth and change. I anxiously watched my first perennial vegetables germinate, checking their health and wellbeing regularly. I watched some growing strongly, others less well and yet others disappearing overnight.

I watched the polycultures as a whole – the way plants grew together, their different shapes and times of growth and retreat. How they nestled together, one growing through another. I watched as one by one other plants seeded themselves in the garden amongst the vegetables and I watched how they behaved, how they got on occupying close quarters with the original plants.

I watched the intricately woven polycultures to look for harmony and synergy developing in the garden. I noticed and noted the clover, vetch or bird's-foot-trefoil that can help with the nitrogen supply in a patch. I could see the potential in the arrival of a new wildflower from a different plant family that would nourish insects not currently provided for. Polyculture eyes see the niches in the garden filling up as biodiversity increases.

I watched for other signs of life and saw birds, spiders, beetles, worms, bees, butterflies, hedgehogs, rabbits, mice, frogs, toads and other wildlings. They were the first indications of an emerging ecosystem. You cannot have an ecosystem without the wild. It is not tame or managed or convenient. This watching is about letting the 'wild' in and seeing what happens.

I watched the bees arrive *en masse* when I first grew phacelia and mustard plants. I watched Scwuffy, my favourite daddy blackbird with his damaged wing, repeatedly and persistently coming to the garden day after day for over two years, hopping round the polyculture patches, digging out worms for his family. I watched blue tits visiting the fennel and devouring the seeds and goldfinches coming for dandelion seed heads. I watched for slugs, but didn't see many, just evidence that they were about.

I watched through the seasons. In winter I watched as the garden withdrew below ground, beneath frost, fog, rain, waiting in silence. I noticed my own corresponding withdrawal from the garden. Not that I had lost interest, I still scanned the garden anxiously to see if my plants would survive frost and snow, but somehow I too needed to stand apart, step aside, spend time in quiet, reflecting, being, writing. At the turn of the year I felt the momentum for change that would come with the impending rumpus of spring.

From late winter onwards I fervently scanned the ground for signs of life re-emerging. There were edibles such as lamb's lettuce, land cress, three-cornered leek, few-flowered leek and the adorable early flowers – snowdrops, crocus, and the inevitable daffodils, each in their turn bringing delight. And as spring became ever more voluptuous I watched it explode into summer, with even more growth and yet more delicious edibles and delightful flowers. After the first burst of summer it continued to roll in, replacing the wild abundance of spring with a more measured wave of colour, but I always noticed a huge surge of growth as summer drew to a close.

I noticed in each season that some days hold a precursor of what is coming next. There were January days when the light was bright and clear and I could smell spring coming. Some days were too warm too soon, bringing early insects to the newly opened flowers, prefiguring the eventual coming of summer. There were summer days that held a hint of autumn in the air, maybe the howl of an August storm threatening to blow in an early autumn. There was the premature chill of winter on a cold autumn day and the memory of the wet and cold that was to come.

I watched beauty unfold. As I stood back and let nature take its own course there was an ever-increasing range and number of flowers. They were often incredibly numerous – too numerous to count – fragile, delicate and amazingly beautiful.

In short, I watched everything. From their first surreptitious peek above the ground to their final decomposition I saw the whole of the plants' lives.

what does this mean?

In this pause, this abstention from activity, this precious time of waiting and of watching, you begin to notice things and that will lead towards understanding them. It is not the work of a few minutes or hours or days or even months. It is an ongoing and a forever thing, a cumulative experience of me plus the garden which equals more than the sum of the parts. Watching engages us with what we watch. It stimulates enquiry as I ask what is happening, why and how? It fosters the development of concern and care and of empathy and eventually it gives birth to thoughtful, insightful, intuitive and even playful participation.

So I have waited and watched. I have observed and thought and researched. I have taken hundreds of photos, made pages of notes and written dozens of posts on my blog[5]. Because of this I have much more of a sense of the garden as a whole, as well as the individual plants in it, than I did before. I am more grounded, more focussed, more centred. By biding my time I have developed patience and resisted the impulse to control. I am entering into relationship with this patch of land and its plants and animals. I will be much better placed to make wiser, ecosystem-centred, life-centred decisions than I was before. I have eschewed a formulaic approach for a living and dynamic knowing. It is not possible to emphasise enough how important this is. It is vital to see what actually happens, to counter the received wisdoms of our culture and our human prejudices.

wilding your understanding in the pause

What else is happening in the pause? Is all the waiting, watching, noticing and letting go achieving anything else? Everything I see is being stored up ready for my understanding to maybe catch up with what the garden and its inhabitants are doing. They are not

---

[5] annisveggies.wordpress.com

destroying my initial handiwork in planting the garden but they are in fact weaving their own infinitely better structure. All this underlines the fact that I am not the leader and the garden has no hierarchy, I am but one part of a circular and webbed network of relationships.

Pausing and not being sure about what is happening means there is room for review, time to learn and to watch and to evaluate, to think and then to do things differently – room for openness and room for possibilities to unfurl. This is the start of wilding (or possibly re-wilding if you prefer) your understanding and beyond that it is the very faintest glimmer of beginning to wild or to re-wild your heart and soul. It is also the start of seeing things differently and of beginning to reclassify old terms and dispense with prejudices. Plants no longer fit into conveniently labelled categories and there is no longer cultivated versus wild or invasive plants; there is no longer either good or bad, right or wrong. There are no longer pests, and although there will be a lot of exuberant plants growing and spreading around, this is neither messy nor overgrown. As I watched my first forest garden I stopped disliking weeds and made friends with the wildflowers instead. It didn't happen overnight and the cultural conditioning of the first five decades of my life have ensured that the old instincts continue to emerge unbidden. I think it is hard, perhaps impossible, for experience to override this (probably indelible) imprint on the psyche.

waiting

Whilst you are watching all of this you are of course simultaneously waiting. Waiting and watching, watching and waiting – they are inseparable twins. Waiting is guaranteed to be uncomfortable. Indeed such passivity can be profoundly disturbing. From of old, gardeners have disturbed their gardens, now is the time for gardens to disturb their gardeners! But it is this theatre of experience that leads to all the valuable lessons. Here are some of the things I have watched whilst I waited to see what would happen next. Each of them led to something delightful that will be explained in more detail in the following chapters.

A plant appears that I did not plant. It could be a 'weed' (herb robert or bittercress) or a self-seeded edible plant (leaf beet). It could be herbal (wild marjoram) or floral (calendula) or something I do not know ...

Dock plants have set themselves in one polyculture bed and stinging nettles and buttercups in another bed ...

Two plants that I planted and definitely want – maybe oca and tree onions – start to grow very close together ...

Nasturtiums that self-seeded from last year have a growth spurt after the late summer rains that amounts to a tidal surge across the garden, covering several feet in a short space of time and covering skirret and onion plants beneath themselves ...

Radish or parsley, being widely regarded as annual plants, come to the point where they are 'normally' harvested or removed ...

Dandelions grow and flower ...

I plant four or five different varieties of mint in the long border ...

Plants flower and run to seed, the neighbours point out that my flowers need dead-heading ...

It is early autumn and my neighbours are tidying up, cutting their plants back ...

A mass of minute seedlings of edibles like lamb's lettuce or land cress germinates ...

A large honesty plant growing up against a fence and therefore out of the wind drops its seeds on the ground directly underneath where it stands, and a mass of seedlings germinate later that year ...

Eggs and/or caterpillars appear on the perennial kale leaves and on the mashua – this will always happen every year in the end ...

Rabbits visit the garden and eat their fill of the newly emerging greens. Pheasants are there too eating the seeds I have sown ...

I find slugs in amongst the greens ...

I see snails in the plants, on the path, in the bushes ...

A burdock plant grows up through a mass of parsley or wild marjoram ...

... I do nothing. I watch and wait.

At a time in history when all our former certainties about how the world is or should be or will be are gradually (or not so gradually) abandoning us, now is the time to come to terms with flexibility and uncertainty, to learn to dance with life, experiment, wait and see, be patient, do things differently. Here then is a precious opportunity that is almost always overlooked. Pausing is the prerequisite – abstaining from action and then, in that pause, hand-in-hand come the twin sisters of watching and waiting, or if you prefer, waiting and watching. Neither precludes nor precedes the other – they come together or they don't come at all.

only do the minimum

principle 5

When you have to do something, only do the minimum

why does the forest gardener only do the minimum?

I didn't even ask myself this question to begin with. I had in effect undertaken to do only the minimum right from the outset because I was trying to emulate Fukuoka's natural farming model and thereby to save myself time and effort. Nevertheless this question needs an answer that goes beyond such self-centred concerns. I now understand the answer to be that by keeping yourself out you let nature in.

So after stopping, watching, waiting and doing nothing, when the time comes to act, what is next? If there are so many tried and tested and familiar gardening tasks that are no longer applicable, what is to be done and why? How will the forest gardener decide upon what to do? Is this not all too vague and airy fairy to be practical? How do we integrate ourselves into the ecosystem in practice? What does this actually mean?

Reiterating principle number 3, it means that *everything* the forest gardener *does* takes *full account* of the forest garden ecosystem past, present and future. Forest gardening is an interaction between the forest gardener, the forest garden and the living natural world both within the garden and close to it. It is between the two extremes of a completely natural (wild) place and a totally controlled (human) landscape. However, in terms of what happens within the garden it is not located at a half way point between these two extremes, but much closer to the wild end. The forest gardener needs to understand that nature will attend to all the really important functions of the ecosystem thereby making the forest garden healthy, fertile and abundant, with a living soil. Our role is to support these processes, avoiding the reflexive responses of horticultural convention, learning to gently guide the direction of the garden in line with our own purpose and vision. We need to learn to garden with the forest.

principles in action

Because a forest garden is intended to be a self-perpetuating ecosystem, permission for it to evolve naturally is encoded in its design and planting. The forest gardener has relinquished responsibility for forcing the garden into a chosen mould and trying to ensure that the 'right' things happen. So we must accept the consequences of the forest garden having this freedom and accept that much of what happens will be out of our control. We must realise that plants may be eaten or die because of this. We will stand in our place as part of the garden but not its controller and accept what comes and learn to get along with the consequences. The garden has its own path to follow and we have the freedom to travel with it on our joint path of discovery.

This is not easy at first. Accepting freedom and opening up to what that means in a forest garden is very unfamiliar territory. It is one thing to say that we will put aside control and start to trust nature and it is another thing entirely to do so. Because it shows up very starkly just how much the story of human dominance and control is written into our lives from our earliest days. It means we need to change the thoughts and habits of a lifetime, both in the garden and beyond.

One of the joys, as well as the challenges, is opening up to new possibilities and opportunities, learning to trust nature and to continually deepen that trust. It is part of learning a new way to be a gardener and eventually part of learning a new way to be a human being. It challenges our patience, our adaptability and our inventiveness but it also deepens our understanding and encourages us to develop polyculture eyes, polyculture mind and eventually a polyculture heart.

nature's initiative

This requires a lot of un-learning and new learning. It is about sensitivity and empathy, encouraging and supporting the connections that hold the forest garden ecosystem together, rather than wrenching them apart or creating obstacles to its functioning. Nature is continually taking the initiative and trying to add more plants into the garden, and the forest gardener is learning how to fit in with the developing ecosystem and to merge with its activity, so they are complementing and not contradicting it.

We need to understand that forest gardens work because of their internal ecology and their links to the ecology of their neighbourhood via visiting insects, birds and mammals. Everything about their structure, their functions and their benefits derives from this fact. Therefore, all aspects of their design, their planting and subsequent care must link fundamentally to this ecology and allow for natural processes to do much of the work conventionally done by the gardener. The forest garden principles guide, support and enable the gardener to trust the garden and to make ecologically sensitive decisions.

As described in previous chapters, when I began my first forest garden I had already read, re-read and absorbed a lot of information. I was ready and prepared to look for plants that filled more niches and for more animals that did too. I was alert to the benefits of more flowers from as many plant families as possible and which flowered for as many months as possible, so I took care to watch for new plants that could do this. I knew more biomass would feed the soil so I allowed plants to grow as much as I felt comfortable with before reacting. I knew that more fertility came from perennial plantings, increased organic matter in the soil and increasingly active soil life. I knew that greater abundance was the product of a healthy, fertile garden and I trusted what I had learned was right and so I was able to let these things happen.

But I still had to put this generalised understanding into practice in real life. Referring back to the scenarios from chapter 7, let me explain what I did, why and how.

> **A plant appears that I did not plant. It could be a 'weed' (herb robert or bittercress) or a self-seeded edible plant (leaf beet). It could be herbal (wild marjoram) or floral (calendula) or something I do not know. I do nothing; I watch and wait.**

Herb robert is a wildflower in the geranium family with pretty pink flowers. It spreads by sending out runners sideways and establishing a new plant – rather like strawberries do. If the ground is fertile it rapidly grows larger, sending out a lot of new runners, straddling neighbouring plants and covering them. Initially I am happy to leave herb robert alone if it is filling in an otherwise unoccupied space and thereby adding to the local diversity. However, once it starts to get larger (about one foot tall) and clamber over other plants I take it out. It is loosely connected to the soil, or sometimes not rooted at all, but presumably feeding through its connections to neighbouring plants. It pulls up very easily. Having pulled up a plant I put it on the ground near where it grew. I know more herb robert will grow, it is not eradicated, nor do I want it to be.

Bittercress is a very small ground-hugging plant that appears very early in the year – often in January or even in December if the weather is mild. It is usually considered by gardeners to be a very difficult weed because the seed pods pop and shower seeds around, potentially making lots of new plants. In my old gardening days I used to remove it assiduously but it kept on returning – probably because I kept disturbing the ground by removing it. However now I know that bittercress is edible and although it has a strong flavour it is not bitter. I may pick a small amount to go in a winter green salad, but mostly I will leave it alone, and paradoxically I no longer have a problem with it. Now that most of the ground is covered with either plants or mulch and is not disturbed by digging or weeding there is much less opportunity for bittercress to spread as it once did. It is an annual plant and dies back quickly after setting seed. Because it is small, bittercress doesn't add much biomass, though it will attract very early and tiny pollinators and fills an otherwise vacant niche in the ecosystem.

Plants that just arrived – salsify and nasturtiums – growing amongst onions and skirret

Leaf beet is a pleasant tasting, leafy green edible and perennial plant. It belongs to the *Chenopodiaceae* family (like beetroot and chard) and after flowering produces a great many seeds. Of these, only a few germinate and I am always happy to see new seedlings. I respect that new plants are growing in the best place for them and leave them to grow on to maturity. Additional leaf beet plants mean more edibles, more biomass and more diversity. Even if we ate all the leaves, the root system remains below ground and is interacting with the unseen part of the ecosystem and benefiting the soil.

Wild marjoram is a herb and one of my very favourite plants because it is so remarkably attractive to bees. I welcome it wherever it sets itself and will rarely remove it unless it is interfering with another plant that was there first or if it grows too large for the space it has occupied. Calendula is also welcome. It is bright and cheery, edible, medicinal, easy to grow and generally a compact plant that fits in between other plants quite nicely.

Any new but unplanned plant – whether wild or cultivated – represents potentially more biodiversity or more biomass; or perhaps both. Of course, very many new and unplanned plants appear in any garden and this is definitely a continuing test of the intention to watch and wait. If I don't know what a new plant is, the first thing I do is to identify it and then find out:

* What are its benefits? Is it edible or medicinal?
* What is its potential role in the garden ecosystem?
* Does it fix nitrogen?
* What is its root system like?
* Are the flowers attractive to bees or other insects?
* How is it propagated or how much is it likely to spread?
* Is it growing at a time of year when not much else is?
* What does it do when I leave it alone and watch and wait?

This is one way to embrace biodiversity – seeing the practical advantages that each new arrival brings and the answers to these questions help me decide whether or not a particular plant is likely to benefit the garden. In general, my presumption is that, because this plant has grown there in the first place, it is probably filling a niche in the ecosystem even if I am not yet sure what that is!

So, almost always I leave well alone – at least to begin with. However, if at some future time I think a plant is not proving beneficial to the overall garden system I will remove part or all of it. If it is small I will pull the whole plant up. If it has or is likely to have a large root system I will usually cut it off at ground level as it is too disruptive to pull or dig it up. Most annual plants will die when this happens to them and leaving the roots in place below ground means that when they decompose or are eaten, channels tracking their former course will remain below ground, allowing for movement of water, air, and small creatures too. However perennials are more likely to sprout again from the base like the dock plants in the next example.

but what about really bad weeds?

Experience makes me much less anxious about this question but I am aware that there can be great fear among gardeners of weeds running amok, of disorder, and of the garden being taken over by what tend to be known as thuggish plants. It is true that if plants are proven to be counterproductive to the overall health of the ecosystem, or to the forest gardener's purposes and vision, they will need to be wholly or partially removed.

Do not be overly concerned about this. Forest gardeners are looking for stability and balance and this we will get as long as we hold fast to actions that support and enhance the whole ecosystem. How we make these decisions changes over time. We start out knowing or thinking or believing certain things, but what we know, think or believe alters subtly all the time as our polyculture eyes absorb more of how the natural world behaves.

My observation is that most wild plants have many potential roles within an ecosystem. Those listed in the table overleaf all seeded themselves in the garden and between them are accomplishing a whole host of useful things.

Plant	Bee and insect plants	Biomass	Capturing minerals	Climbers	Ground cover	Habitat	Nitrogen fixers
Bird's-foot-trefoil	✓						✓
Cleavers				✓		✓	
Clover	✓				✓		✓
Cowslip	✓				✓		
Creeping jenny					✓	✓	
Dandelion	✓	✓	✓				
Dead nettles	✓				✓		
Evening primrose	✓	✓	✓				
Forget-me-not	✓					✓	
Foxglove	✓	✓	✓				
Fumitory				✓		✓	
Greater celandine	✓	✓	✓				
Ground ivy	✓				✓	✓	
Honesty	✓	✓	✓				
Purple toadflax	✓					✓	
Scarlet pimpernel					✓		
Self heal	✓				✓		
Speedwell	✓				✓		
Sweet woodruff	✓				✓		
Thistle	✓	✓	✓				
Vetch species				✓			✓
Willowherb	✓	✓	✓				

Dock plants have set themselves in one polyculture bed and stinging nettles and buttercups in another bed. I do nothing; I watch and wait.

Dock plants are not commonly permitted in gardens! They grow large and if I am honest I didn't really want them but they are here and I am bound to my principle of doing the minimum. What I do is to take off the leaves when they get too big for where they are growing and to always take off flower stalks when they appear. Docks are vigorous and their leaves grow fast and the flower stalks keep on coming, but all this is biomass and the leaves are likely to have stored minerals in them, so this is actually a very fresh and continual green manure feed for the soil. After a while I started to look for a purpose beyond this in them and I can see now that they are nature's way of breaking up the soil, using their strong and deep tap roots to drill down through the hard, stony ground. I saw a small copper butterfly in the garden this week for the first time and have now discovered that sorrel and dock are its larval food plants. In similar fashion to dock plants, other generally despised plants with persistent roots including dandelion and hogweed have become an everlasting source of green manure. Hogweed has sap that can cause a very irritating or even burning rash if it gets on the skin and is exposed to sunlight so I am careful when close to it, but it is fine in the hedge where it feeds plenty of insects throughout the summer. I understand that hogweed seeds make a delightful spice, but I have to admit that I haven't tried them yet.

This garden was once a field and buttercups have probably grown here forever. They are well suited to the heavy damp clay in the bottom corner of the garden and it is no surprise that they find their way from the lawn and into the polyculture bed. I am quite happy with buttercups in the lawn, they are okay growing around the perimeter of the bed and the fruit bushes can co-exist with these strong plants. But I have found that it is best to pull out any buttercups that start to grow across the polyculture bed because they smother many of the herbaceous edibles like Good King Henry, wild strawberries and perennial leeks.

Stinging nettles have plentiful uses – they are edible and medicinal and for the suitably intrepid and determined they can be used for dyes and fibres. They accumulate lots of minerals and donate these minerals back to the humus in the soil if they are used as a mulch. They are also food for the caterpillars of red admiral, small tortoiseshell, peacock and painted lady butterflies all of which have been abundant this summer. But then again they do sting! I got used to being stung by them a long time ago and have been in the habit of leaving them as much as possible for all their wildlife advantages and also for biomass. However more recently they have in some places become very strongly established and, due to rising levels of fertility in the whole garden, they have grown more than I really wanted. Another consideration is that we have a number of young grandchildren who spend time in the garden and the plan is that they enjoy it and not that they grab a nettle and get stung. So with those considerations in mind I am removing the nettles from the polyculture beds and I can safely let them grow huge in the hedge!

Having intervened to pull up or cut off part or all of a plant or plants what does the forest gardener then do with the plant material in their hand? What is a minimal action? From the outset what I took it to mean was that I would never dispose of surplus plants in the conventional way, such as on a compost heap or in a green bin for collection. Instead I would simply to do what nature would do – place them on the ground as close as possible to where they grew to feed the soil right there. Very occasionally this is not possible for practical or aesthetic reasons but almost always I do it this way. I have always called this mulching in place, but I have also found out there is a permaculture term for it which is 'chop and drop'.

This simple activity, mirroring the actions of nature saves a whole load of work making compost and I cannot emphasise enough that this is what makes all the difference to the way the garden grows. I know the very suggestion could possibly bring alarm – not least because of what the visual effects might be – but you would actually be surprised that it is not a big deal. It is important to say here that the lush growth generated by this way of feeding the soil soon physically hides the dead or dying plant material that I have placed on the soil surface.

The layer of dead and dying vegetable material forms a mulch on the surface of the soil. It feeds the worms and other chewers and the soil bacteria too. It keeps the soil protected from summer heat and winter cold, holds in moisture, protects the soil from heavy battering rain and is a home for many valuable spiders and beetles, etc. Leaving plants to go to seed potentially means lots of unwanted seedlings – the thick layer of mulch prevents too many from germinating.

And this all makes sense of the principle to do the minimum. I never need to export potential fertility from the garden via the green bin or council waste site, nor go to the additional effort of making compost when nature does everything necessary just where things are.

Sometimes there is simply more plant material than can be physically accommodated close at hand. But I always find somewhere to put it – in my previous garden it was beneath the tall shrubs and bushes and in my current garden this is usually in a pile on a polyculture bed, which is not the same as making a compost heap. It is just placing plant material in a pile close to where it grew, it not structured and it is not turned. At some point I will distribute the heap around the adjacent plants or more widely over the soil during the winter as a protective mulch again. It always stays as close as possible to where it originally grew. I have noticed ever increasing numbers of beneficial insects year on year and now I am wondering whether these heaps of mulch are also perhaps heaps of habitat – giving insects and perhaps other creatures both food and a place to keep sheltered during the winter.

There are other types of biomass as well – cuttings from the lawn every week or so during the summer, prunings from both the hedges and some large branches sawn from the mixed hedge. Lawn cuttings go directly onto the garden. They are not always that pretty but they soon disappear either because the summer sun dries them out or because the other plants grow to cover them. There have never been any problems resulting from doing this, although I am sure in a less well-balanced ecology this would be slug heaven.

I have an admission to make here. Sometimes we have a gardener to take off the top growth that we can't reach on the *leylandii* hedge and he takes those cuttings off site. If my partner has cut this hedge we put the trimmings on the garden. We do half of the mixed hedge each. Usually the trimmings generated go on the garden, but sometimes (and sshhh – don't tell anyone!) the trimmings go across the lane to the woodland next door. This is in fact closer to where they grew than the other side of our garden and in nature's terms is part of the same ecosystem, but I guess the woodland owner may not like it.

One part of the mixed hedge had lots of very old and dead branches lying horizontally across it from when it had been laid years ago. It seems that the branches in the hedge at that time were cut through too deeply before being bent down in the laid hedge and they never survived that treatment. So there were a lot of long, horizontal but totally rotten branches in the hedge when we moved in. I have been able to remove them gradually and use them in the garden sometimes beneath new beds I was making and sometimes to form an edge for these beds. The hedge also generates a lot of surplus growth every spring and summer and these long and bendy stems can be used either to make a type of woven edge round the deep beds, or for sticks for climbers.

Other branches I needed to remove were chopped up and put round the fruit trees and bushes as a woody mulch to encourage mycorrhizal fungi to grow. I have seen the white strands of mycelium developing beneath these mulched areas indicating the fungal network growing and spreading. If there was no room left beneath the fruit trees, they were put at the base of the hedge to be used as a woody mulch sometime in the future. Sometimes this has meant a very large amount of woody materials at the base of the hedge – mostly on the roadside edge and not visible to us. Once again this is heaps of habitat for lots of overwintering creatures which I am sure is of enormous benefit.

When I need them, I will retrieve branches and twigs from the piles under the hedge. I break up saved twigs or branches and scatter them in some of the polyculture beds for more texture in the soil and

I use smaller twigs as sticks to support peas and beans and as visual indicators of new plants I want to keep an eye on.

Before moving on, I have another confession to make – that I did indeed use a compost bin in the first forest garden. But after I converted it to a forest garden I only put in vegetable peelings, etc. from the kitchen and shredded paper and some cardboard. When the bin was full, I just tipped it on the garden and spread out what had decomposed and put the rest back. Now in Wales the local authority collects the kitchen waste and I use paper I previously would have shredded to light the fire.

what about overcrowding?

> **Two plants that I planted and definitely want – maybe oca and tree onions – start to grow very close together. I do nothing; I watch and wait.**

These two crops were growing in a deep and fertile polyculture. Oca is a root crop which produces floppy and succulent foliage and which responds to high fertility with more top growth. Tree onions grow very well in the same conditions, making tall sturdy plants. I had not anticipated that the oca would grow so much and spill across close to the tree onions. However, the onions were not affected by this incursion and I left everything alone until it was time to harvest the oca – some went to the kitchen and the remainder was replanted further away.

> **Nasturtiums that self-seeded from last year have a growth spurt after the late summer rains that amounts to a tidal surge across the garden, covering several feet in a short space of time and covering skirret and onion plants beneath themselves. I do nothing; I watch and wait.**

Nasturtiums surging across the polyculture bed

As the forest garden matures it can generate far more prolific growth than the gardener has witnessed before. Such an astonishing surge of growth, maybe after a period of warmth and good rain can even feel a bit scary as though it is un-natural. Perhaps that is the point? Maybe it is not un-natural, but rather it might be thought of as hyper-natural – a phenomenon that nature has generated but which is beyond our own previous experience. I think it is entirely possible that because we continually thwart nature's capacity for abundance we don't actually know, nor can we imagine, the extent of what such abundance might be.

I am becoming accustomed to larger and larger plants and also to abundant harvests. The kales and onions have been prolific for some years, but it has taken some time for the fruit bushes to mature. Finally, this year they were absolutely smothered in blossom and then in currants. The fruit trees are only just starting to mature sufficiently to bear fruit but the indications from those that have begun are that harvests will be plentiful.

This year the jostaberry bushes grew far more than I have ever seen before – there was an incredible amount of growth on each one and I cut an average of 40 two-foot stems off each bush in early summer to prevent them from getting humungous and outgrowing their space.

gardening with the forest

principle 3 continued

Everything the forest gardener does takes full account of the whole of the forest garden ecosystem – what has happened, what is happening and what they intend for the future

This is the other side of the story. So far we have been considering what happens when we watch, wait and do the minimum, allowing nature to effectively take the lead in the forest garden. I deliberately put that first to emphasise the fact that we are not controlling this process. However the forest gardener has their own legitimate goals for the forest garden, and these can be changed as necessary, in response to what happens, as long as we remember to do so in a sensitive and considerate way.

Gardeners – of every description – are well known for hankering after new plants and in the context of the forest garden there are plenty of novel edible trees, shrubs, bushes and herbaceous perennials to experiment with. Then there are the plants you are given by friends and family and those you just want to have because you love them. The forest gardener is a valuable member of this ecosystem, their needs and wants as valid as all others. There is most definitely a role for intelligent, sensitive and thoughtful introductions of new plants as time goes by and as long as you continually bear in mind the needs of the whole garden ecosystem – the need for diversity of function, plentiful niches for wildlife and plants to benefit the soil you will find places for all of them.

From amongst the original plantings some of my precious plants have either died or failed to thrive. Sometimes the cause has been exceptionally harsh or atypical weather conditions and in other cases I had just tried a plant that was not suitable for this location. The perennial vegetable casualties include ulluco (a root vegetable), various alliums including Chinese chives and nodding onion. Some annuals I had hoped would become self-seeding on a continuing basis such as carrot and parsnip did not do so. They grew well the first year but their freely falling seeds did not manage to set again for the next season. I did not interfere by saving the seeds myself and sowing them, but left it all to nature. Because of the changes inherent in the garden becoming dominated by perennial plants it seems that unless they are wild annuals do not thrive here after a while.

Then there are human reasons for making changes. Maybe you need to change some structural aspect of the garden – the route of a path, a new outbuilding, a change to a fence or wall. Maybe you want to try more new and unusual trees and plants. I am continuing to create and enlarge the polyculture beds and experiment with different edibles and flowering plants as my vision for the garden evolves alongside my understanding of it.

Change comes for many reasons, but it is continual, and what you see this year may never happen again which means that we have to continually be alert to the processes or stages the garden is undergoing. And all the while the forest gardener is watching and waiting and they are asking "what does the garden need at this point?" This is when vision slips gently alongside and holds our hand and whispers, "more biomass, more butterflies, more trees, more flowers, less work".

tiny fruit trees

Before long I realised that this garden was best at growing fruit and green vegetables. In the second year I planted four heritage Welsh fruit trees – damson Abergwyngregyn, cherry Cariad, plum Denbigh and apple Trwyn Mochyn – and one variety that is supposed to do well just across the border in Shropshire – apple Sunset. Cherry Cariad is in the triangle border and the other four are across the garden spread between the polyculture beds.

The following year I decided to put in as many fruit trees as possible, planting into the long border, and this time I did not buy heritage or local varieties but chose what I fancied eating – cherry Morello, pears Concorde and Invincible, gage Reine Claude de Bavay, mirabelles Ruby and Golden and quince Vranja.

Apple Sunset

I came upon a method of growing tiny fruit trees, promoted by Ann Ralph that does not depend on the rootstock to keep the trees small and is said to work with any rootstock. The most important thing is the first pruning, which is then backed up with a particular pruning style that keeps the tree tiny – I am aiming for no more than my head height. Keeping trees deliberately small could be construed as very controlling – and therefore contrary to my clearly stated intentions. In an ideal world I would allow them to grow more naturally but this is my compromise in order to achieve diversity of both plants and harvests. It has enabled me to increase the variety of fruit and include more from the plum/gage family that I wanted to try.

The year after, I realised there was room for fan-trained and step-over fruit trees along the border with next door and planted Red

Falstaff apple as a fan-trained tree, and two pears and another apple as step-overs. The next year, I decided to really push the little tree method and planted more, squeezing them in between the heritage trees in the polyculture beds and planting one in the long border to replace a casualty. This time I focussed on fruit I wanted to eat but I also tried to ensure that they were reasonably likely to be happy here – apples Newton Wonder and Bramley, gages Cambridge and Denniston's Superb, plums Marjorie's Seedling and Victoria, cherry Stella and a medlar.

The trees are all young still and it will take a few years to see if I have pushed this concept too far. There have already been a few casualties – the Abergwyngregyn damson, golden mirabelle and Reine Claude de Bavay gage. The damson was my fault because it didn't like the pruning I gave it when I cut it back to the tiny fruit tree size in its second year. If I had done it at the outset I think it might have been fine as it had begun to fruit before it died. I think that drought could have been part of the difficulty as well. The other two were French varieties that really didn't like the Welsh weather which was probably predictable from the start! As I write it is early January, the early snowdrops are flowering on a sunny bank in the local wood whilst in my garden the ruby mirabelle is also starting to flower. This is way too early, but we are having a mild winter and it has got ahead of the calendar. The golden gage did precisely this a few years ago and was then caught by the frost; first a whole branch died back and then the rest of the tree followed.

abundance

In return for this planting, having given the garden what it needs to become fertile and healthy, we are rewarded by a garden teeming with life and becoming ever more abundant. Despite the casualties mentioned above nine of the fruit trees have begun to bear fruit. Thus far, indications are generally of good crops of healthy, tasty fruit. In years to come the other trees will begin to bear fruit and even if there were only 2kg per tree that would be well over 40kg in a season. There are at least 17 currant and berry bushes and three sets of raspberry canes. Apart from the newest raspberries, these all produced heavily last summer. One whitecurrant bush alone bore 2kg of berries. If the fruit bushes continue to produce at this level there is the potential for as much soft fruit as tree fruit.

I have been leaving some plants to live out multiple life cycles and to reproduce themselves hoping to exchange smaller harvests now for greater harvests in the future. Plants in the onion family including perennial leek, three-cornered leek, few-flowered leek, wild garlic, Welsh onion, tree onion, chives, garlic and more grow well here and after waiting a few years for them to multiply I hope to be able to start harvesting more this year. In due course I would like to provide all our garlic, onion greens and leeks and a good proportion of bulb onions from the garden – whilst not by any means taking all that there is.

All the kale plants are huge and I can harvest as much as I want most of the year and the neighbours help themselves (with permission!) as well.

I have refrained from harvesting many of the root vegetables for a few years as I have been leaving them to open up and effectively dig the soil for me. These include Jerusalem artichoke, Chinese artichoke, skirret, oca, burdock, salsify and scorzonera. Mashua is a root vegetable that I don't much like the taste of, but it is an attractive climbing plant with flowers in November or even December; this is sprawling up the hedge and will feed late autumn insects. Earth nut pea is a nitrogen fixer that is multiplying and spreading through the long border. At some point the waiting will be over and some at least will be dug up and eaten. Roots are always a surprise; you can't tell in advance what is there below ground, although judging by the amount of leafy growth there is there should be plenty hidden there.

adapting to becoming a different gardener

A forest garden relies on natural processes to develop its health and fertility. It requires the gardener's acknowledgement that nature knows better than we do and can very easily accomplish the outcomes we once tried to achieve through control. Refraining from

Daubenton's kale (foreground), giant kale flowering (centre ground) with self-seeded honesty (centre left)

intervention is putting this understanding into practice – testing out that you do actually and fully believe it. You will soon enough learn how deeply conditioned we have been by our culture to want to control at every opportunity.

Be aware of the disturbance, the discomfort visited upon you when you cannot automatically remove a weed or cut a vigorous plant back or dead-head something that has gone over. Be clear that this is a process of unsettlement. You are being uprooted from your previously assured place at the top of the evolutionary tree and being replanted in a much smaller niche, lower down the order of things (as you would previously have understood it) – much lower down. But also be clear that this refashioning in the order of things, shapes you into a being that fits better into your own forest garden niche where you increasingly feel at home.

Forest gardening is immersion in how nature operates, immersion in nature itself to learn from personal experience. The forest gardener becomes increasingly adept at seeing the garden as a whole and also of weighing up the different roles and contributions of each part. The nitty-gritty of making decisions rests on these abilities. It all comes with practice, and watching, waiting and doing the minimum is the only way to learn. Some actions may become almost routine, but never actually routine. They may be repeated because it makes sense at that time for all the reasons above – but nothing is ever done automatically and without thinking.

One of the chief joys of forest gardening, of participating in a living system as a partner and not as a controller, is to enjoy this dance with the natural world. Nothing is set in stone and the forest gardener decides in a deeply reflective and respectful manner. Every gardener will make their own decisions. This is as it should be; it is how things work in this different world. There is no right and no wrong, just things as they are and the way forward opening up afresh all the time. With hindsight there will inevitably be times when you wish you had done differently. However, as a natural creature playing about in a natural way in the world, you will have an effect. That might be the effect you intended or one you did not intend. Either way it feeds into the whole cycle of watching and waiting, pausing, doing the minimum and gardening with the forest.

A bird does not have a plan about how it does what it does in making a nest, mating, rearing young, feeding itself and its family. It has instinctive patterns of behaviour – ways to find food – but the blackbird visiting my garden does not single out a particular worm for breakfast, nor does the thrush choose a specific snail to feed to its baby. The worm and snail that are eaten are just those that happen to be there at that time. In similar ways, what I choose to do or not to do in the garden is an outcome of me and the configuration of plants and other creatures that occur at any one time.

To engage in this way with a forest garden is to open up a boundless cascade of possibilities as the gardener and garden settle down into a relationship, with each plant much freer to follow its own course, flowering, multiplying, maybe feeding and sheltering wildlife, perhaps feeding the humans and inevitably eventually feeding the soil. There is no way to predict what will happen in the space of a single summer, and giving this freedom to the garden ensures both vitality and surprises.

But what about the feelings of conflict that continue to arise with the garden and with oneself? Think and read about what is going on. Look back at notes you may have made or photographs taken. Take a breather. The garden is almost certainly trying to head in a direction that you do want, albeit by a route you are not familiar with. It will naturally increase in fertility, biomass and health and we need to learn to recognise this. Know your plants, know your niches, know yourself! The garden will take its cues from the gardener. If you want a relaxing garden, become a relaxed gardener, don't ask, 'what do I want to achieve?' Instead ask, 'who am I?'

The temptation to make clumsy, large-scale, heavy-handed interventions lessens and the forest gardener is increasingly content with mere tweaks. Not that the impulse to intervene more strongly ever goes away, and perhaps the urge to control never fully dissipates. When faced with a garden that is full of flower heads gone over and lots of rampant new growth after a period of warmth and rain in late spring, I can remember and still feel the impulse to 'tidy up' and thereby to control and to subjugate. But I don't do it. I am sure sometimes I do more than my more enlightened intuitive self would like, but old habits not only die hard; they maybe never die.

Nature makes its moves and I make some of my own, cautiously, carefully, thoughtfully – always with the greater good of the garden and the wider environment in mind. Nature dances and I learn its dance. I set a direction of travel and then follow rather than lead.

it all depends

Objectivity is society's preferred choice for making decisions – standing apart, assessing, calculating. But if we want to cede control in the forest garden, we will need another approach.

The opposite of objectivity is of course subjectivity, but we tend to treat this as though it is not a valid way of making decisions. But think about it – do I really want to make decisions from a place of heartlessness; cold calculations made dispassionately from an isolated, disconnected point of view? Let us embrace subjectivity because, as well as our individual blind spots, we each have our own truth and our own intelligence, our own guiding lights.

Learning to trust our natural subjectivity comes through experience and is felt in the heart and the soul. It is experienced when we are caught up in play, in fun, creativity, passion, beauty, art, dancing, joy; when we feel connected, interconnected, woven together, enmeshed, complete, part of the whole and not separate from it.

the wisdom of it all

If I dug or weeded I would have a weed problem. If I thinned plants out I would have less diversity, less biomass, less beauty, less health and fertility and more weeds. If I dead-headed plants, the birds would have no seeds for the winter and there would be none left to set themselves growing in unusual places, nor would the insects have anywhere to spend the winter. If I spent more time doing these things – that is to say working – I would have less time to spend watching and thinking and enjoying. There would be less habitat for all sorts of animals, the ecosystem would be impoverished and less abundant. Everything would be diminished, me included. Instead both the garden and I are enriched.

polyfloral polycultures

principle 6

Plant polyfloral polycultures everywhere

This principle is about having *thousands* of flowers, in flower, everywhere for as much of the year as possible, because flowers are *absolutely vit*al to the full expression of the ecosystem of a forest garden. By the term *polyfloral* I mean plants that bear thousands of tiny flowers either all at once or over a period of time. Some of these will be wild plants, others will be well known garden plants or herbs and vegetables that are not conventionally permitted to flower. Very few are plants actually recommended in garden centres or seed catalogues as beneficial for bees and other insects. So by the term *polyfloral polyculture* I mean a mixed planting that covers the functions needed in an ecosystem, to which are added plants bearing vast numbers of flowers.

From the outset I knew I had to include flowers as sources of pollen and nectar, but it took me years to understand more fully their vital importance. As with everything else I have learned, it happened in the pause as refraining from intervening, watching and waiting led me to some unexpected learning. I was particularly surprised by the revelation that many vegetables and herbs are the most outstanding flowering plants.

In that prolonged pause, plants that do not flower in conventionally managed gardens came into flower. This is not because the plants themselves are necessarily unusual, but because they do not usually stay long enough in a garden to flower. The plants in question include wildflowers, both perennial and annual vegetables, herbs, the onion family (alliums), green manures and nitrogen fixers from the pea and bean family.

For a perennial plant, flowering is the culmination of its annual growth and for an annual plant it is the prelude to seed production and death. Flowers need pollinating and insects need food – and the more flowers, the more insects. A forest garden is, and needs to be, a haven for insects of all kinds to live, feed and to reproduce.

To explain more about this, I want to briefly describe the life cycle of a bumble bee as I have learned it from a fascinating book entitled *A Sting in the Tale* by Dave Goulson. The bumble bee year begins as early as February or March when the queens emerge. At this point they have been hibernating since the previous July and are nearly starved and desperately need to find spring flowers to feed from. I have certainly seen some very early bees on bright and warm spring days that feel much too soon and even in my polyflorous garden there would be precious little apart from spring bulbs for them to visit this early on. Goulson suggests that pussy willows are one of the few plants to flower this early and that small trees can attract hundreds of hungry queen bumble bees. The queens that are able to find food fatten up and the eggs develop within them.

Many bumble bee species like to nest below ground but are poor diggers and need to find holes already dug by mice, voles, moles, etc. After finding a suitable site, the queen constructs a nest and lays eggs which are fertilised as she lays them using sperm she has stored within her body! The eggs are then incubated and need to be kept at about 30°C at all times despite often sub-zero temperatures outside the nest. The queen shivers to generate heat and, as Goulson (p.24) explains

> shivering uses lots of energy which is why the queen has already placed her pot of honey within easy reach while she sits on the eggs; but this is not enough to keep her going for long. If she leaves her eggs for too long to collect more nectar they will get cold, but if she does not go to fetch food she will starve. _A queen may use her own weight in sugar each day to incubate her brood, which may necessitate visiting up to 6000 flowers._ If these flowers are too few and far between she will be away from the nest for much of the day, her brood will cool and as a result develop too slowly, and she will wear herself out in her frantic search for food. _Hence the proximity of lots of nectar-rich spring flowers is probably vital._ (emphasis added).

After hatching and metamorphosing the first young bees to emerge are female worker bees that then feed the queen who remains within the nest being cared for. Again, as Goulson explains:

> after a few exploratory trips they start to range further, and experiment with visiting flowers. They have innate preferences for blues and yellows, so will tend to visit flowers of these colours first. Finding nectar and pollen in flowers, and learning to gather it efficiently is harder than it might at first appear, and it takes a few days for the worker bees to perfect their skills. Once they have, however, food begins to flow rapidly into the nest, and the queen starts to lay batches of eggs more regularly.

All being well over time the number of worker bees grows significantly and later on the queen begins to lay eggs that will become future queens and others that will be males. New queens and males spend a few days resting and feeding on honey and pollen before seeking each other out for mating. Goulson notes that in high summer males seem to be very common:

> they sit around on flowers drinking nectar; they prefer flowers with big, sturdy heads such as thistles and knapweeds, and gangs of males can often be seen clustered together.

The male bees die at the end of summer and the queens look for somewhere – preferably just below ground – to hibernate. They need to be fat and to have chosen a good site. Small or inadequately fed queen bees will not survive hibernation and others will die from becoming mouldy in damp weather or being drowned by heavy rain. So it is hardly surprising that, by the time that spring comes round again, few of the mated queens are still alive to emerge and start foraging for food.

There has been a huge amount of publicity these past few years about the plight of the honeybee and more recognition has more recently been given to the vital role of the bumble bee. I hope that this brief trip through the bumble bee year will help us all to understand more about the necessity of trying to support them too in our gardens – be they forest gardens or any other kind – and to this end Dave Goulson founded the Bumblebee Conservation Trust.[6]

Once I discovered that the early queen bumble bees need thousands of flowers to forage from, I understood why many native trees and plants bear massive numbers of flowers early in the year. So forget the large showy blooms of cultivated flowers, what is required are thousands upon thousands of exquisite, tiny flowers. Watching the garden I saw bees and other insects utilising flowers most of the year. As well as seeing the very early queen bumble bees in March, I have also seen red admiral butterflies, wasps and flies on the ivy flowers in November. And afterwards dead flowers and seed heads make great structures for overwintering insect homes and eventually everything is simply more biomass.

The first flowers I really noticed *en masse* were the green manures phacelia and mustard. Convention and the seed packet instruct that they be dug into the soil before they flower. Of course, I didn't do that! I left them to flower and was struck by the large number of bees they attracted. Over time, as I will describe below, I saw carrots, fennel, marjoram, sweet cicely, forget-me-nots and lots of other plants flower like this.

> **Radish and flat-leaved parsley, being widely regarded as annual plants, come to the point where they are normally harvested or removed. I do nothing; I watch and wait.**

I scattered a pack of free radish seeds in a space in a polyculture bed one summer. I did not harvest the roots as they did not grow much, whereas the top growth was far more than I had ever seen on a radish. I let them produce their simple four leafed pale mauve flowers and subsequently set seed. When the plants had died back I laid them on the ground beside their former growing place to decompose *in situ* and feed the soil.

---

[6] https://www.bumblebeeconservation.org/

I was doing this with the other plants as well and the fertility must have been increasing in the polyculture bed because the second generation of radish plants grew huge – as high as my shoulder and several feet across! They were growing amongst fairly burly plants – Jerusalem artichokes, yacon and mashua – and these gigantic radishes fitted in well. Although their blooms are individually small and apparently insignificant, the sheer size of these plants created large clouds of blooms which appeared as a pale purple haze across the garden. Visitors, having never seen anything like this before, repeatedly asked what they were only to be very surprised by the answer. As well as looking lovely, the radish flowers like others in the brassica family taste nice – much milder than you might expect and young radish pods are hotter but quite tasty too.

Huge, self-seeded radish plants flowering

As well as looking gorgeous, the flowers were attractive to many insects including cabbage white butterflies. They may even have been decoying the cabbage whites away from the kale plants but I couldn't be sure about this. I wondered about growing them specifically to try to do this but after a couple of years fewer radishes germinated and the plants were not as large as before. I cannot be sure why this was – maybe the fertility was different, maybe rainfall was different that year, perhaps the polyculture bed was becoming more suited to perennial plants than to annuals. I miss these lovely flowers but, in the end, I don't need to know why they went nor to try to coerce them to grow again. There is a time for everything.

Forget parsley as a bit of greenery on the side of a plate for decoration or even as a more important part of the cooking. Flat-leaved parsley is *definitely* for flowers – it has been an absolute delight.

I bought one plant for the Telford garden and left it in place at the end of the season. It lived through the first winter and set seed in its second summer. Some of those seedlings were transferred to the Welsh forest garden and the following year they in turn flowered and set seed, drifting down the garden (but paradoxically against the wind) to the newly planted triangle bed. There they germinated that same year and produced so much leaf that I was considering trying parsley cooked as a green vegetable, although I never actually got round to that. The plants also made a very attractive counterfoil to the surrounding plants. The next summer they flowered and what a display they made – it was the most stupendously amazing, beautiful, dazzling display, an utterly transfixing sight – flower heads with uncountable numbers of perfect tiny white flowers. I could apologise for the superlatives, but I'm not exaggerating. This was an absolutely wondrous display which was alive with insects all summer long. What raptures I enjoyed!

Flat-leaved parsley in full flower

Dandelions grow and flower. I do nothing; I watch and wait.

In my traditional gardening days I once paid my children to take the flowering heads off a mass of dandelions to prevent them spreading in the garden. These days, now that I don't disturb the soil, dandelions don't spread much. They are one of the earliest flowers of the year and they are beloved by bees which need all the forage they can get in those early weeks of spring. Dandelion flowers are in fact very beautiful and the whole plant is also edible and has medicinal properties. Try chewing a young, but nevertheless very bitter, dandelion leaf if you are suffering from indigestion.

I plant four or five different varieties of mint in the long border. I do nothing; I watch and wait.

I know, of course, that in conventional gardening, planting mint anywhere other than in a pot is asking for trouble. Maybe that's why I did it! I planted them with several varieties of thyme, germander and hyssop as a herbal edge to the long border. I don't know why but none of the mint plants in my previous garden had spread into the surrounding space and I was very interested to see what happened here. The plants varied in their vigour but they all grew outwards and starting spreading into their neighbours and closer to the fruit trees than I wanted them. In this case I think I watched and waited a bit too long! Most of the mint plants had put out a lot of roots below ground – further than I had anticipated – and I am now removing most of them.

Perhaps the crucial difference between this garden and the previous one is that mint planted in my former garden had to adjust to grow within an established network of trees, shrubs and bushes, etc., whereas in this garden it was in more or less virgin territory, with nothing much to hold it back. I am not trying to eradicate it, but to bring it into a more appropriate balance with the trees and bushes that are now more established than when the mint was first planted.

What I did find out though was that mint is a wonderful bee plant. It blooms from the bottom of the flower stalk to the top and therefore lasts for weeks during which time it is covered with hosts of busy bees.

how many flowers are there?

I have tried counting the flowers on some plants and when I quickly exceeded the number I was prepared to count to I tried calculating the approximate numbers. Here are some of those calculations. The first one is for fennel. On one radial flower head there were seven tiny stalks each bearing about 20 tiny flowers – that is 140 flowers per head. There were five of these heads on a stem which makes 700 flowers and in turn there were three of these stems on the main stem – that is 2,100 flowers. The multi-stemmed plant had five of these stems, which makes 10,500 flowers on the plant. There are at least ten fennel plants in the garden which makes a total of 105,000 tiny fennel flowers.

Wild marjoram flowers from July to September. It has masses of tiny flowers ranging from white to pink to mauve which are covered in legions of insects. It readily self-seeds and can appear anywhere in the garden. One small sprig of marjoram had 24 flowers and there were eight sprigs on the stem which makes 192 flowers per stem and with approximately 300 flowering stems in the bed that makes 57,600 flowers.

Fennel in full flower

connections with other places

Dandelions, radish and parsley are just the tip of the iceberg as far as attracting insects is concerned. One by one these humble plants showed me that they shared a strong bond with the insects which flocked to them – different insects for different flowers. Bees and butterflies seem to visit a range of different flowers, but some of the less common flowers such as parsley or carrot are smothered with tiny insects that appear to the unaided eye to be all the same on each plant. These were insects I had not seen before and it seems that they had come to visit specific flowers. And all this raises questions.

It would seem as though potentially thousands of insects visit the garden and seeing such a massive upsurge in the number and variety of insect pollinators visiting the flowers I began to wonder where they had come from. Had they been lurking close by just waiting for these particular flowers? Had they travelled a long distance to visit them? Either way, where would they have found food if they had not had these flowers in my garden? Or did they breed here in my garden? Where else do they find food? What about their other needs, for that matter how many other places do the insects that come here need in order to complete their own lives and start the next generation?

I don't know the answers, but it makes me realise that each tiny fly or beetle that most of us will never even see and still less know anything about, needs a place to live and to eat and to reproduce and to die. We may well know about bees and butterflies, but everything in nature is intimately linked and if there are no flowers for less well known or less 'glamorous' insects, then they will die. As Dave Goulson says – quoting biologist E. O. Wilson – *"if all mankind were to disappear the world would regenerate back to the rich state of equilibrium that existed ten thousand years ago. If insects were to vanish, the environment would collapse into chaos."*

Just asking the questions demonstrates to me that my garden is not an isolated ecosystem, but that it is intimately and fundamentally connected to many other places by the insect visitors – and also the birds and animals as well. These places in turn will be connected to many others and this is the reality of the network of nature –

everything is vitally connected to everything else. I think of my garden as one minute fragment of a huge number of nested ecosystems that ultimately cover the whole planet. And even a bit of thinking about this shows quite clearly that we need to reinforce these living links and do everything we can to stop breaking them apart.

Planting polyfloral polycultures everywhere, then, is a means of creating further opportunities for nature to increase the complexity of the web of life in this place. The details of nature's intricate links lie beyond my comprehension but we can easily understand that our actions can support its activity and thereby increase the resilience and health of the forest garden. Equally we need to be aware that our actions can, unfortunately, easily do the opposite. I like to think that, in their own way, the insects that visit my garden appreciate the flowers on offer for them. But how much better would it be to have thousands and thousands of similar places.

beauty and the human side of flowers

Flowers bring smiles, people light up, they stop, pay attention, admire, talk and even marvel. There is no need to explain this effect, flowers are a universal language. Given as tokens of love, empathy, congratulations, celebrations, appreciation, in memory and in sympathy – they cross the entire range of human experience and emotion and we understand what they are telling us. Don't worry, we're here. We can bring you joy, even now.

All of the polyfloral flowers I grow are supremely joyful flowers. The way the flower heads are constructed from virtually uncountable numbers of minute individual flowers and multiplied into the thousands on a single stem is both intriguing and delightful to me. Add to that the visitors buzzing around and it seems to me that nothing gladdens my heart or lifts my spirits faster than the sight of literally thousands of minute flowers alive and seething with uncountable numbers of bees and other flying creatures. The name 'the garden of delights' first sprang to mind when I saw the flat-leaved parsley and many other flowers buzzing with insects all day long and all summer long (and as I will explain in due course, the 'equal' part of the garden's name came later on).

my other favourite polyfloral flowers

I could enthuse more or less endlessly about very many lovely polyfloral flowers. Personally I like the apiaceae family best – including those already mentioned – fennel, carrot and parsley plus angelica, sweet cicely, valerian and skirret. Here are a few more details about some of these and other favourites.

Ivy has flowers late in the year – from October onwards – on stems that have grown high and bushy. It attracts lots of flies and wasps, but also and much more colourfully, on sunny days it is smothered with red admiral butterflies. This summer there have been holly blue butterflies in the garden which came to rest on the ivy. I found out

Carrots in flower

from my reference book that the larvae of the second brood of holly blues may feed on ivy – which seems plausible. I have never even seen a blue butterfly anywhere before so I am really happy! Later on there will be ivy berries which feed the birds through winter and spring and come the spring there is often a tit family nesting in it as well.

Carrot is an exceptional flower, I would go so far as to say an exceptionally exceptional flower. Bearing uncountable miniscule white flowers arranged in umbels across a flat face, it has all the intricacy of a very fine lace. Each head is breathtakingly beautiful, and as there are several heads on most stems, they cluster together and magnify the effect. As they go over and start to form their seeds the whole structure folds up into an elegant egg shape. Wild carrot is lovely as well.

Salsify is a simple pink daisy flower. It is elegant and perfectly formed in small clusters atop elegant (and edible) foliage. Beautiful as the flower is, the seed head surpasses it for simple loveliness. Bees love the flowers.

Field beans have beautiful flowers – in an understated kind of way. They vary from cream to pale beige or pink and are marbled with black having a different pattern on each flower. They flower from late winter to late spring but may not attract pollinators until later on as they never seem to set pods until May or June.

And last but not least here are a few others I don't want to miss out:

* Wildflowers – forget-me-not, scabious, primrose, foxgloves, teasel, violets, cowslips, snowdrops
* Perennial and annual vegetables – chives, Welsh onion, wild garlic, burdock, cardoon, Jerusalem artichoke, mashua, lamb's lettuce
Herbs – sage, lavender, thyme, hyssop, angelica, elecampane, catmint
* Green manures – buckwheat, phacelia

* Garden flowers – love-in-a-mist, Californian poppy, bee balm, calendula, stocks, phlox, honesty, hollyhocks, honeysuckle
* Nitrogen fixers – wild vetches, bird's-foot-trefoil, clover, earth nut pea
* Trees and bushes – hawthorn, apples, pears, currants, elder, blackthorn

To emphasise my growing fascination with polyfloral flowers I wrote two blog posts about the flowers and insects. In May 2016 I estimated that there were 12,500 forget-me-not flowers, at least 800 flowers on each mature lamb's lettuce and each sweet cicely, and 1,200 flowers on 60 mustard flower heads.

Lamb's lettuce flowering amidst chives and Welsh onions

I didn't attempt to estimate the additional flowers on the aubretia, bugle, honesty, erisymum, land cress, dandelions, daisies and blackthorn, nor the apple and cherry blossom nor the flowers on jostaberries, gooseberries and various currants. There were at least 15,000 flowers on the plants I did estimate which is far more than I had expected and importantly each one is potential food for insects of all kinds with plenty more to come as the year moves on.

In March of the following year I wrote about fennel, carrot, angelica and sweet cicely:

Of course having a large number of polyfloral plants is one part of ensuring biodiversity in the forest garden and perhaps this is just a particularly clear example of the benefits of biodiversity feeding and housing lots of different insects and birds.

I don't need to say any more – just be sure to plant polyfloral polycultures everywhere. Please.

life cycle gardening

principle 7

As far as possible the trees and plants in a forest garden should live for their full life span, and reproduce themselves naturally and unaided

In a forest garden, the trees and plants mostly live for the entirety of their natural lives. Whereas in a conventional garden we have learned to cut those lives short, to control and interfere in the name of tidiness, hygiene, convention, aesthetics, more harvests or quicker harvests, efficiency, respectability and general 'good management'. What a shame.

Everything that has been discussed thus far – pausing, watching, waiting, doing the minimum and polyfloral polycultures – means the gardener is not interfering with natural life cycles and the plants are freed to follow their own course. Whether they were planted by me or they have appeared unbidden they grow, flower, bear their fruits or seeds and die according to their own inner nature. In particular it was flowers that first awakened me to life cycles.

> **Plants flower and run to seed, the neighbours point out that my flowers need dead-heading. I do nothing; I watch and wait.**

I didn't have any difficulty ignoring the horticultural injunction to dead-head and by this point the neighbours knew me well enough to expect just that. Polyculture eyes noticed many plants managing their own life cycles – salsify, burdock, wild garlic and wild leeks, poppies, sweet cicely, calendula and more seeding themselves into tiny gaps and flourishing there. Watching this, polyculture mind recognised the endlessness of the cycle of life. It was another delight to see natural processes of reproduction happening year after year with no need of my assistance.

It is early autumn and my neighbours are tidying up, cutting their plants back. I do nothing; I watch and wait.

Of course, by practice and convention gardeners cut back or remove plants that have finished flowering or perhaps just gone past what is deemed to be their best. I do cut plants back eventually but not until late spring by which time the need for winter habitat and nesting materials has passed and new growth is springing from the ground. The physical architecture of the dried-up stems and stalks and seed heads provides many tiny nooks and crannies for insects to hide away in. Some of the material may come in handy for nesting birds in the spring and leaves will fall to the ground and provide a cover of mulch until it is digested by the soil organisms. Fennel, which had been so adored by the insects through the summer surprised me as I watched blue tits arriving in droves early one autumn morning to feed on the seeds. There were so many seeds that they came to feast for weeks if not months.

A mass of minute seedlings of edibles like lamb's lettuce or land cress germinates. I do nothing; I watch and wait.

At any time from autumn to late winter patches of self-sown lamb's lettuce appear. Uncountable tiny plants are all crammed in together and at first the plants are far too small to pick up never mind eat. Once I can actually pick a plant I start to take very small harvests. I pick as often as I need to from this time onwards as the plants continue to grow but there are so many I only ever have a fraction of the total. Eventually, usually in late April or May, they make a really rapid growth spurt ready for flowering and by this time there are far fewer plants. Even though I always mean to watch very closely with my polyculture eyes I never seem to quite spot the transition from a mass of small plants to many fewer and larger plants – I am not here all the time though, so maybe it always happens when I'm away! At this point I stop harvesting altogether and let the flowers develop and seeds ripen. After this the plants die back, decompose and rapidly disappear into the soil where they once grew. I have sometimes saved the seeds, but be warned, if you do this, that they smell appalling! Now I leave them to scatter where they will and as a result there are more and more patches of lamb's lettuce every year.

Land cress does the same as lamb's lettuce – starting from a mass of tiny seedlings and ending up with just a few plants. It is a very strong tasting plant, akin to watercress, so I only ever take small amounts. By the time they produce a tall flower shoot, the plants are often quite sizeable with large leaves and both flower shoot and leaves are better cooked than eaten raw. I am often surprised where the new patches arrive, but even if I don't want or need to eat them they are a good early flowering plant for the bees.

A large honesty plant growing up against a fence and therefore out of the wind drops its seeds on the ground directly underneath where it stands and a mass of seedlings germinate later that year. I do nothing; I watch and wait.

As with the lamb's lettuce and land cress, many fewer plants make it to maturity than started out. From this honesty plant I got the idea of using it purposefully as a green manure. I lay the mature stems with the ripe seeds still attached on the ground where there is a gap somewhere that I think is appropriate. They germinate and make small plants that year or the following spring and grow larger and flower in their second year. They are lovely early spring flowers for the bees and the plants are food for the caterpillars of the orange-tip butterfly.

Gardeners usually sow seed thinly or evenly or both but nature does it very differently. More often than not nature is extravagant and irregular, and apparent over-production is a frequent occurrence – think tadpoles, fish eggs, caterpillars, etc. Small beings are very vulnerable and so there are very many more at the outset than will get to the end. Otherwise they would not survive at all. Seeds are no different.

I used to save and scatter some seeds myself and sometimes I still save some, usually to share with other gardeners; the rest are left for the birds and the wind to take. Nature sows them where it will. There is no way of predicting for certain which plants will reappear the following year and the composition of flowering plants constantly changes. One year calendula, poppies and polemium grew very strongly, another year it was love-in-a-mist, burdock and marjoram. This is just the way the ecosystem matures and as it does so it produces spontaneous combinations of flowers that are often very beautiful.

Honesty, forget-me-nots and dandelions growing with tree onions and elder

'appropriate' intervention

Although there is a lot of autonomy for the forest garden ecosystem it is nevertheless not a wild place. Many plants can look after themselves, but some will always need support from the forest gardener in order to reproduce.

perennial kales

I think of perennial kales as one of the stalwart perennial vegetables. I currently have both plain green and variegated Daubenton's kales and Taunton Deane, none of which flower, and another kale plant that came to me originally as 'wild kale' which doesn't look like true wild kales and which does flower. Some sources say that flowering stops kales being perennial but in my experience after flowering they continue growing just as before. If you try to stop them flowering, they continue to produce ever smaller flower shoots in a desperate attempt to fulfil nature's destiny. I think that this is what may weaken the plant and that it is preferable to let them flower when they want to, without interference. Having said that, there is no harm in harvesting some of the flowering stalks, when they are young, as broccoli substitutes.

Kale plants tend to get tall and leggy and often collapse under their own weight. In line with my non-interference policy, I allow them to do that, letting them spread out and I think that they are spontaneously layering themselves – that is generating new roots where the stems touch the ground.

Daubenton's and Taunton Deane kales have a multi-branched structure and Daubenton's in particular has uncountable numbers of side shoots. I use these to make cuttings, usually in spring or autumn, but potentially at any time of year. Cuttings can be popped into a pot or directly into the ground, depending on the incidence of slugs. I put mine in the ground directly now and enough of them make it to maturity to keep a supply of new plants either for the garden or to share. Sometimes I take a sizeable side shoot to eat the leaves and then use the remaining stem and a couple of small leaves as a cutting.

The plant I first knew as wild kale grows very large and produces masses of seed. These don't tend to germinate spontaneously in the garden, so I do save them to share and also to sow in spring if I need more plants.

onions (alliums)

Onion family plants reproduce by one or more of the following – by seed, bulbils or bulb division. Hard neck garlic varieties produce 'scapes' – tiny bulbils on the top of what looks like a flower stalk. Tree onions and perennial leeks also produce bulbils. I may remove the leek bulbils before they ripen to use in the kitchen as a garlic substitute and to allow the plant to direct its energy to the below ground bulb division. Those that remain to maturity can be planted and in so doing I can mix them up with other plants across the garden rather than have them all grouping together. I let wild garlic, few-flowered leek and three-cornered leek send their seeds where they will, but sometimes dig up a clump to colonise another part of the garden or to share. When Welsh onions and tree onions make large clumps, I also divide them and move some to another area. Harvesting and eating can also be part of this digging up and replanting.

root vegetables

The tuberous plants I grow – oca, mashua, earth nut pea, *Apios americana*, Jerusalem artichoke, Chinese artichoke – are generally left where they are and they can usually look after their own life cycles. For the past two or three years I have not harvested them in order to let them both multiply and also to 'dig' the stony soil for me. The plants die back in autumn-winter and reappear in the spring-summer. However, it is getting to the point where I need to harvest and eat some of them and move some others. The Jerusalem artichokes need moving because they are encroaching on some of the fruit trees. I also need to make sure the Chinese artichokes and *Apios americana* are in places where they do well, and to check the earth nut pea is not swamped by fennel and fruit bushes.

Bulbils forming atop tree onions

Salsify would not grow in the Telford garden but I managed to get a single plant to take in my first polyculture bed in Wales. Since then I have done nothing towards helping it grow or reproduce, but it likes this garden so much that it is everywhere. One year I counted well over a hundred small plants in the long border by late summer. I removed one or two to show visitors their roots but left the rest and a year later there were perhaps a couple of dozen plants remaining. Whether they were eaten or just died and decomposed I don't know but nature took what it took and left what it left. This cycle has continued year after year. I value the flowers immensely for their beauty and for the bees and I adore the seed heads for their even more wondrous symmetry. The flowering shoots at the stage of swelling before the buds appear are edible and very nice cooked but cannot be harvested if you want the flowers!

Salsify seed head

Skirret is a perennial root vegetable that makes new baby plants close to the original plant, and when this happens I move the babies to new places.

fruit bushes and trees

These generally require conventional management. Currant and berry bushes need to stay more or less within their allotted spaces; jostaberries in particular grow large and start to grow across other plants; gooseberries are less vigorous but it is practical to keep their spiny encroachments out of the way. I always use some of what I prune from fruit bushes as cuttings to make more bushes and I do this at any time of year. I cut the prunings into six- to ten-inch lengths and push them into the soil in the nearest convenient location.

Sometimes this is right by the parent bush other times it is elsewhere in the garden. I either use the new plants in the garden or give them away.

Following advice gained on a course with Martin Crawford of the Dartington Forest Garden, I let raspberries run where they will. I cut them down or tie them up if they physically get in the way of the path or the bins (which is one place they grow). They are never in a cage or shelter of any kind and I don't cut them down as recommended in conventional gardening. I just let them be what they are and most years there is a fabulous harvest.

Of course some plants can never reproduce themselves and this will be the case with the tiny fruit trees. There will be no other way than to buy replacements when they are needed.

life cycles and life cycling

Leaving most plants in the forest garden to live out their lives to a natural end, and to generate their own successive generations, saves a lot of work. It also respects the integrity and capability of the ecosystem.

Nature turns in cycles and circles, it has rhythm and purpose and so must our forest gardens. The growth and maturing of a forest garden is all about keeping the cycles going. An ecosystem flows, it is not cut up, disconnected, disjointed or dismembered on a regular or planned basis, and the forest gardener's role is to promote this flow and, as far as possible, not to disrupt it. The human desire for control that translates itself into the everyday interactions between conventional gardeners and their gardens, interrupts life, continually setting things back to the start point. In that context these interruptions work, and are necessary for growing our everyday vegetables but they have taught us to disregard and to discard the wealth and generosity of the natural world.

Unless there is a very good reason to do so, from the point of view of the forest garden, to remove or cut off a plant before it has reached the end of its natural life is to disempower it, and effectively removes its purpose, its value and its intrinsic worth. A plant's purpose is not fulfilled until it has completed its contribution to the whole, when it has lived its life to the end; after which there is new life from death as other life forms consume its remains. In a forest garden, an ever-increasing diversity of plants and animals are able to complete their natural cycles – die, decompose and dissolve back into the soil to feed other lives in other forms.

This is in effect the corollary of doing the minimum and in practical terms it means not doing conventional gardening tasks like dead-heading flowers that have gone over, cutting back plants before they have died or clearing the ground back to bare soil once the flowers are over or the crop is harvested. It is about leaving nature to do some things that conventional gardeners often particularly dislike, like allowing the seeds from the uncut flower heads to spill, ping or float where they will. Finally, but equally importantly in this garden of equal delights, it also helps to create a stable and healthy environment for many other creatures to live out their own full life cycles where there is food and habitat for them all through the year, but maybe particularly in the cold and inhospitable months.

In sublime moments the forest gardener witnesses the metamorphosis of stick to leafy branch or bud to flower and thence fruit and seed, and finally this year's life mulches down to feed next year's new beginnings. There is always new life emerging and older life retreating. In the end, what every living thing contributes to the circle of life is their own life.

Continuity and renewal are the context for everything in the forest garden and for me. Now is the unfolding of forever and as all the trees and plants in the forest garden live out their own life cycles, generation upon generation, life itself cycles through the garden. This is never-ending. The forest garden has a future continuing into time unknown. Thus it becomes a bridge across time and space as energy and matter cycle repeatedly through all life. The forest garden is a localised part of great global cycles – cycles of carbon, nitrogen, water and more. There are cycles within cycles, all interconnected, melting from one to another in the endlessly productive dance of life. This is a paradox of constant change within continuity, and within it there is a magical element of unpredictability.

The challenge is to learn to live with this, to live with energy and matter – the ultimate constituents of every life – transforming themselves endlessly in a repeating dance. The forest gardener is a dancer too. My place is in that circle of life – alongside you and all life. It always was.

nature's transformational magic

Rabbits, pheasants, caterpillars, butterflies, slugs, snails, aphids, will all come and have some food here

principle 8

Support nature's transformational magic

transformational magic and the ecosystem

Like every other aspect of forest gardening, the principle of supporting nature's transformational magic is embedded in the knowledge and practice of the forest garden as an ecosystem. It follows closely from the last principle, expanding and clarifying some aspects. As forest gardeners we can now see energy and biomass cycling through the garden in ever-changing forms, but are we ready to consider what we previously knew as pests as an equal and utterly necessary part of the garden ecosystem?

Supporting nature's transformational magic is about recognising and enabling what is going on when natural processes or events are transforming one life form into another. Any creatures known as pests generally eat the plants the conventional gardener wants to grow and when they outnumber their predators there can be population explosions. For example, a lack of ladybirds may allow a population explosion of aphids, but labelling the aphids as pests is unnecessary and counterproductive. I have, by the way, only very rarely seen any aphids in either of my forest gardens – and those occasions were last summer when some of the plants were growing at an enormous rate and when there were drought conditions and the plants were all under stress. I didn't take any action and there were no dire consequences.

It is more appropriate in the forest garden to see such occurrences as indicators of imbalance and I want to throw away this word 'pest' which really just describes a manifestation of imbalance. It is the imbalance that is a problem not the creature and they are not to be scorned, dismissed or eliminated. What is needed is time, more variation in available habitats in the garden and thereby the opportunity for biodiversity to increase. There will be fluctuations in the populations of all the creatures in a forest garden over time but in an established and maturing forest garden ecosystem, no single species will come to predominate over the others to such an extent that it causes problems.

If you want to locate the true pests and the prime un-balancers of the ecosystem take a look in the mirror and consider what role you play within natural ecosystems. What you take and what you give, what you leave, what you cherish or destroy and what your actions and activities do in the wider world, have their ripple effect.

The forest gardener needs to lose the culturally conditioned reflex action we all recognise to seeing a slug, a snail or a caterpillar and eventually to learn to welcome all life into the garden as gifts direct from the heart of nature. I learned this through watching and waiting.

Eggs and/or caterpillars appear on the perennial kale leaves and on the mashua – this will always happen every year in the end. I do nothing; I watch and wait.

In my early years of forest gardening I had the usual reflex reaction to seeing first the eggs and then the caterpillars of the large and small white butterflies. I wanted to get rid of them and I either removed the eggs or, if I didn't see them before they hatched, I gathered up the caterpillars. Sometimes I gave up, overwhelmed by the sheer numbers. At one time I wondered about using other plants to decoy the butterflies to lay their eggs elsewhere but that didn't lead anywhere. However, eventually (it really is amazing how long these realisations take!), after years of watching, I had a breakthrough and realised the obvious – that the cabbage white butterfly was part of the local ecosystem (whether I liked it or not) and it needed to be here. As a corollary I also thought that it was conceivable that the kale might even need a degree of munching by the caterpillars.

I think this finally occurred to me because I was settling into a trusting relationship with the garden and with nature as the arbiter of what happens there. Knowing something in your mind is one thing, but knowing it with your heart and therefore being able to trust is quite another. I first became open to the idea of caterpillars being useful or even necessary to my kales one summer when there was a great deal of kale munching going on. I decided to leave things to happen as they would without interference and by the time I went on holiday for a fortnight in September the kale plants were more or less destroyed. Imagine my surprise and delight on returning to find transformed plants, no sign of the crinkly-edged, munched leaves, but regenerated plants with healthy new growth. The same thing happened the following summer, but with me feeling more trusting about the outcome, which was the same – regenerated plants with healthy leaves. This has happened every summer since then. And in a later development I have recently seen blue tits helping themselves to the caterpillar eggs on the underside of the kale leaves. They didn't take them all and the leaves are being well and truly munched outside the window as I write, but it is another indication of the ecosystem maturing.

In his wise and thought-provoking book *The Lost Language of Plants* (p.157) Stephen Harrod Buhner gives a pertinent perspective on the relationships between organisms in the ecosystem:

> *Plants and animals have coevolved over a long period of time and their relationships reflect <u>mutualistic interdependencies that are often millions of years old.</u> Many of the actions of animals when they eat plants (termed "herbivory") are <u>necessary for both plant and ecosystem health</u>. Herbivory alters the density, composition, and health of plant communities through eating plants, dispersing seeds and defecation. Some plants produce an initial series of leaves designed to be eaten, and more luxurious growth only*

appears once that has happened. For many plants, metabolism, respiration, and metabolic transport are all <u>stimulated by animal and insect feeding</u>. It is <u>only after foraging rises above a certain level</u> that many plant defensive compounds are produced in quantity or come into play. (emphasis added)

> **Rabbits visit the garden and eat their fill of the newly emerging greens. Pheasants are there too eating the seeds I have sown. I do nothing; I watch and wait.**

I take no action and, having had some years of practice by this time, I don't find it hard. I have agreed to these constraints, to these happenings, and I see the arrival of new animals as an indication of the ecosystem maturing. Rabbits are taken by the birds of prey, local cats and foxes and are run down on the road. I don't mind feeding them for some of their short lives.

The pheasants are refugees from the local shoot and somehow (given that pheasants on the road have an absolute determination to die) they have had the sense to escape the guns. I initially felt annoyed and frustrated by them eating the seeds I had sown, and tried to stop them, but after a year or so I acquiesced. I don't know for sure but I would imagine that they are also benefitting the garden by scavenging for insects, bugs, grubs, etc., much like chickens would do – and manuring it as they go. One year the pheasants felt so at home that they nested in a polyculture patch at the base of a particularly massive burdock plant and laid seven eggs, although sadly they didn't hatch.

> **I find slugs in amongst the greens. I have learned even with these to do nothing; I watch and wait.**

I have signed up to let slugs be in the garden, although I have to confess that sometimes in the past I have moved particularly large ones to the wood across the road. But these days I rarely even see a large slug. I manage to leave any I do see and I have found that their damage has lessened over time as the ecosystem matures. There was a small pond in my first forest garden with resident frogs and toads and I know they take slugs. I also saw a blackbird with a slug speared on his beak ready to feed his young family and am sure this would not have been the only slug to provide the dinner in the blackbird nest. However I am still mindful that slugs do have a taste for tender young seedlings and if I were to grow new seeds or experimental plants I would make sure these had grown sufficiently and had somewhat tougher stems than slugs like before planting them out.

I see snails in the plants, on the path, in the bushes. I do nothing; I watch and wait.

I really have never minded snails at all; they have always been around and I have never seen much damage resulting from their presence. In late spring there are always lots of snail shells along the path round the house and I keep on crunching on them as I walk round. One day I saw for myself how they got there. A mother thrush was with a baby thrush which looked very young and perhaps had only just fledged from the nest. They were on the path hiding behind an overhanging shrub. I heard a distinct tap, tap, tap and realised that this was mother thrush breaking a snail shell to get at the soft animal within. By doing it with baby thrush by her side she was teaching it how to get its own dinner. And sure enough, within a couple of weeks, when I heard the tap tap tap again, it was baby thrush with the snail in its beak getting dinner for itself.

harvest only enough

In the midst of plenty we have enough

principle 9

Whether in abundance or not, harvest only enough

In late summer, when the year's growth is at a peak, when there are still flowers aplenty buzzing with bees and other flying friends, when the ripening fruit is weighing the branches down and the plants are reaching to their full extent, the garden feels lavish and expansive, extravagant even and full of the promise of harvests both now and in the time to come. It was the lure and promise of such edible abundance that first drew me to forest gardening. More harvests for less work sounded like one of the most intriguing ideas I had ever heard. In other words, it meant a bargain and for years I was drawn to this particular bargain. It was probably my main incentive for trying out forest gardening in the first place and I was very keen to maximise the produce from my garden whilst minimising my own input.

In the early years I meticulously weighed all the harvests and recorded my time spent in the garden, hoping to clearly demonstrate the reality of this bargain. I did indeed find that this 'bargain' was working for me – I was doing very little work in the garden – certainly much less than when it was a conventional garden – and yet there was always something to eat, and at some times of year there was a lot to harvest.

All this was very natural and human and it took me years to question this approach. But eventually I lost interest in weighing and measuring as I started to see things anew. In my garden journal on 14 April 2016 I noted:

This current period from last summer onwards is marking or making such a change. From maximum output for minimum effort – which is a very human centred / selfish way of perceiving – even if it is achieved by 'working with nature'. To an attitude that sees re-feeding nature with some of the harvest as of prime importance, letting some go back is actually working with nature, then letting more and more go back, finding a different kind of balance – we get enough and nature gets enough or nature gets enough and we get enough.

If we have truly been learning our place within the forest garden ecosystem, at some point we must all ask the question – to whom does this plentiful harvest really belong?

even in abundance, harvest only enough

I don't have an example from watching and waiting that unlocked the answer to this question and thus identified this principle. However I think it was the culmination of so much watching and waiting, developing polyculture eyes and polyculture mind that enabled me to understand this. This principle is a logical progression from the previous two principles about life cycle gardening and nature's transformational magic. Unlike a conventional garden, proceeding in linear fashion from planting to harvest and then starting again, the forest garden is a cyclical, enduring ecosystem. All kinds of harvests are being reaped by all kinds of creatures at every place and point in time. As I was able to see the continuity and development of the forest garden and the equality and significance of all the members of its ecosystem I began to understand that the abundance of this garden was not solely for me and that to take all I could, would be to exploit and to plunder it.

Finally I could see that whatever the means of growing – forest gardening or conventional – a landscape loaded with food for humans alone is out of balance in respect of other beings. Every being in the garden has its own needs and each makes its own unique contribution. To be serious about forest gardens as living ecologies intertwined with the greater ecosystem beyond, there must be potential human harvests that are *not taken*, foods not eaten in recognition of the fact that these other beings depend on this place (almost certainly more than we do at the moment) and that they must be fed, and fed well.

in abundance or otherwise

It may well be much easier to leave some harvests for others when we have already harvested plenty for ourselves, than when we have not been able to. But if it is a lean time for the gardener, then in all probability it is a lean time for everyone. At such a time the ecosystem as a whole needs more support, not less. And under no circumstances should a forest gardener ever take *everything* – to do so would result in harm to the very ecosystem that we are supposed to be cherishing.

Of course, I could also add at this point, by way of consolation to the forest gardener mourning their prior claim to the produce from the garden, that there are potentially other harvests from a forest garden of sufficient size or diversity. These include wood, weaving and tying materials, dye and medicinal plants and edible fungi. But that is to miss the point. The same principle applies to these products too: they are for sharing and not solely for us. Taking too much wood, for instance, reduces the food for fungi and other decomposers and could impede the cyclical nature of the forest garden's ecology.

how much is enough?

There is no right answer to this. And no wrong answer either. By this stage I think you should be able to trust your own developing polyculture instincts because ultimately there has to be a true change of heart for the forest gardener to share the garden's abundance with everyone else. I have long thought that the proof of anything we take a stand about is demonstrated by our willingness to pay (in one form or another) for it. The kale is not only for me, the caterpillars need some; the apples are not only for me, the pheasants like them too; the blackberries are beloved by the birds and the slugs like strawberries. Welcome!

Edible abundance – variegated Daubenton's kale, jostaberries,
Good King Henry, perennial leeks and herbs

the garden of equal delights

The garden of equal delights is named specifically for this principle.
Here is the full equality that was previously only hinted at. The
banquet in the garden of equal and edible delights is for every being.
We all have an equal place at nature's table.

part 3

by a different gardener

a forest garden is gardened differently by a different gardener

To plant a forest garden is to plant a seed that will grow to become a forest gardener

by what means did I become a different gardener?

By the way of polyculture eyes, mind and heart. By watching and waiting, stopping, doing the minimum, by way of polyfloral polycultures, by encouraging life to cycle through the garden, by embracing nature's transformational magic and by harvesting only enough. By all these means and with reverence and awe did I become a different gardener, in the process rewilding my understanding and finding my wilder self.

appreciation

principle 10

Demonstrate appreciation in meaningful and tangible ways

As with the previous principle about harvests, I initially struggled to find a way to explain or even to understand for myself what it was in the garden that led me to this principle. And then I realised it was everything I described in chapter 7 on watching and waiting.

When you watch with polyculture eyes you see that forest gardening is about rebalancing, about placing responsibility where it rightly belongs. It is a revaluing of what matters, and what was once taken utterly for granted (or worse) becomes precious, significant and vitally important. The forest gardener is released from responsibility, restored to a relationship and can relax in a more appropriate role. To become a forest gardener is to revalue everything in the forest garden and potentially to revalue everything outside it as well.

Appreciation must be felt before it can be demonstrated, and this is another lesson in the slow school of polyculture learning. It is a human tendency to believe we have accomplished certain things – like growing food – without ever acknowledging the vital, but easily overlooked, help and support offered freely by nature. If there is a good crop of apples this coming summer I could say that I grew them. Certainly I would have said that in the past. Or, I could say that along with the sun, the wind, the soil and the bees, I grew them. But naming the most obvious co-creators would only be the start – apples (and everything else in the garden) are the 'fruit' of *the whole garden ecosystem*.

There are degrees of revaluing, and of understanding what our debt is to the natural world, culminating in the ability to identify with and to apply this principle. Just as we may nudge our children or grandchildren towards being more appreciative and perhaps chide them for lack of thankfulness or insincerity, we need to take ourselves to task and begin to truly and deeply appreciate many aspects of what life brings to us that at present we are not even aware of.

functional and useful

I set out to become a forest gardener with the understanding that plants are both functional and useful and that these properties could be utilised to my advantage in a forest garden. It was a self-centred approach and part of my mentality of the time of wanting a bargain. But given the culture I grew up in and obviously still live in, such an attitude was completely understandable.

Appreciation built slowly with my growing understanding of the fledgling ecosystem and over time I began to put together a more comprehensive picture of what was going on in my garden. It went something like this:

Plants are extraordinarily useful and both dead and alive they perform a huge range of different functions within a forest garden. Using the energy of sunlight to photosynthesise, they convert carbon dioxide and water to glucose which is used to build their own structure. Plants are a primary food source for all vegetarian and omnivorous creatures, which in their turn are eaten by carnivores, whilst residual dead and dying plant material is consumed by much smaller organisms. This further translation of the sun's energy represents the generation – by plants – of fuel for virtually all animal and fungal life.

Plants feed from the soil and they also both feed and protect it. Leaf fall, plant die back, falling trees and branches cover the soil with an organic layer of mulch, which protects it from extremes of heat and cold, keeps moisture in, feeds the microscopic animals that live within and provides a home for beetles and spiders and many others. Plant roots are sensitive to the bacteria living in close proximity in the soil and exude sugars to feed and encourage the specific bacteria that help to protect them from harm. Plant roots frequently associate with mycorrhizal fungi and can obtain nutrients from them whilst also symbiotically feeding the fungi the nutrients they require. Mycorrhizae form a network to distribute nutrients and water across large distances; this includes moving them from areas of plenty to areas of scarcity.

When plants die or are cut back, some of their root mass is correspondingly shed into the soil. This feeds the decomposers of the world. Fungi break down woody materials into smaller constituent parts whilst bacteria and others feast on the non-woody materials. Eventually humus – the organic remnants in the soil – is created, boosting soil fertility by enabling it to hold onto minerals and make them available in the future. All these processes are greatly enhanced by the presence of perennial plants whose roots continue to feed the soil food web all year round.

Plants are vital to balancing the flow of water across and through the land. They cover and shade the land and help prevent excess evaporation. Some trees can pump water up from deep below ground and share it with their neighbours. They hold moisture in their physical bodies and, in large numbers in forests, they can regulate rainfall. The physical bodies of plants and trees provide shelter and habitat for a huge variety of creatures, from tiny spiders living in old seed heads to large mammals that sleep in trees. Flowers produce nectar and pollen to feed to bees, butterflies, moths and many other insects and link into the wider ecosystem.

In addition to these crucially important, but somewhat obvious, functions that make a practical difference to the forest gardener, plants do thousands of other things all day every day that contribute to the vital balance of the living world. The manifold capabilities of plants and their sensitivity to and interaction with the rest of life are incredibly complex and intricate and are utterly invisible to us but can be measured with specialist equipment. Stephen Harrod Buhner writes about these relationships in *The Lost Language of Plants* (p.145). As well as the simple carbohydrate molecules that plants make, they also manufacture:

> *hundreds of thousands, perhaps millions of other, complex, secondary compounds: 'acids, aldehydes, cyanogenic glycosides, thiocyanates, lactones, coumarins, quinones, flavonoids, tannins,*

alkaloids, terpenoids, steroids' and more. Adding to the complexity, all these compounds can be made using different metabolic pathways ... and each family of secondary metabolites can contain incredible numbers of substance ... More than 10,000 alkaloids, 20,000 terpenoids and 8,000 polyphenols are known and one new alkaloid is identified each day.

Even though many of these compounds are present only in parts per million or even parts per billion or trillion, they exert significant bioactivity ... Through complex feedback loops, plants constantly sense what is happening in the world around them and, in response, vary the numbers, combinations and amounts of phytochemicals they make.

Buhner then goes on to list the 128 phytochemicals that were found in a single yarrow plant before spending a number of pages detailing the incredible complexities of a plant's journey from seed to fully grown plant. He explains how plants generate hundreds of compounds to protect themselves from being overconsumed by insects and animals and that some plants produce an initial series of leaves that are intended to be eaten – because this feeding is actually beneficial for the plant and stimulates its metabolism, respiration and transportation systems. After a certain point the plant produces deterrent chemicals to stop the feeding. Plants are so highly attuned to their environment and circumstances that they continually use environmental information to determine what phytochemicals to make and in what combination.

revaluing the functional and the useful

The sophistication and precision with which plants do all they do is truly awe inspiring. Without plants, there would just be inert minerals in solid rock, water, airborne gaseous elements and no life. It is plants that weave these isolated ingredients into the web of all life. However it was both understandable and necessary that to begin with I engaged with the trees and plants in my garden in terms of their functions and therefore their use to me and the forest garden. It was the key to entering their world and to understanding it and I thought in terms of functions for a long time. In many ways it would still be easier to think in terms of function, because that is how I have always thought of the rest of the world; it is part of the conditioning of being human. However, thinking in terms of functions and usefulness is not a key to finding your way further into the garden.

homage to all plants

Eventually my understanding progressed towards a deeper appreciation of the complex abilities of plants and the delicate precision of their relationships, and as I became more integrated within my own forest garden it dawned on me with ever greater impact just how much we owe to plants. Plants are mediators of transformation on a global scale; they are the weavers and connectors of the living and non-living elements binding everything together. I have become deeply uncomfortable with thinking of, or describing, plants (merely) in terms of their functions. Even if you deeply admire and love trees and plants, and spend much of your time devoted to them and their wellbeing, to see them in terms of their usefulness and to use them purely as functional entities is to make these amazing, gracious beings into servants. Of course that is the prevailing view.

Seeing and using plants solely for their functions and their usefulness is, in this revalued world, like valuing your family and friends only for what they do for you. So that, beyond their utility to you, there is no appreciation or love or any reciprocity at all. It sounds appalling, doesn't it? That is how we treat the whole of the wider world – as though it is just there for us humans to take, to have, to own, to eat and to mess up and to destroy. Even those of us who claim to love the natural world and try our best to protect it, still have this attitude: it is ingrained in us and not about to be rooted out any time soon.

I would love all gardeners to be able to recognise all plants as precious and valuable and to end the discrimination that is one of gardening's accepted wisdoms. Some are deemed useful, some are edible and tasty, some are beautiful; some are weeds and some are even designated noxious or thugs, and I would like an end to this. All plants are special. From the tiniest to the most massive they are all wonderful and generous beings. It is the human eye and mind that separates, classifies and accordingly approves, ignores or rejects particular plants. These views are the basis of how we treat (manage) the plant world, cultivating a very few plants on an industrial scale, persecuting others virtually out of existence and all sorts of positions in between. Of course, I used to share these perceptions and I used to treat plants in the same way. Take a view from any other place on the planet, through non-human eyes, and you can see relationships rather than functions, and after a while I began to see them that way as well. Time spent in my garden opened my eyes and mind to a deeper appreciation which I call my 'homage to all plants'. I have deliberately used an old and unfamiliar word in an attempt to get to the heart of my altered experience of being a gardener edging my way towards fresh understanding.

Homage is an old-fashioned word which is defined by the Oxford online dictionary as "special honour or respect shown publicly". Some other definitions relate homage to a medieval serf acknowledging the lordship of their master and it can also have religious connotations in showing worship or deep respect to a deity.

So my 'homage to all plants' is in recognition of all that plants are and it is my way of acknowledging a very deep respect and appreciation for *all plants*; my way of saying that I am deeply indebted to them – in many more ways than I can ever know. What an amazing repertoire belongs to the world of trees and plants. How profound are their life-giving relationships that even now keep our world in food and in balance. Deep respect to you all. I pay homage.

revaluing the living world all around

Becoming so much more appreciative has profound implications for the forest gardener's interaction with, and relationship with, their forest garden. Pausing, watching, waiting, letting go, seeing with polyculture eyes and starting to understand with polyculture mind completely reconfigures the forest gardener's values, and rearranges our viewpoint and priorities. The change from selfish, uncaring, unconcerned use of the natural world with, at best, scant understanding of our debt to life, to a deep and respectful homage to that natural world is a monumental journey. This is what I mean by revaluing. Like polyculture learning, of which it is a part, it happens very slowly.

Having paid my homage to all plants in all their forms and with their infinitely varied abilities, now it is also time to pay homage to all other living beings that find themselves in my garden, and in fact all those outside it as well. It means revaluing the wilder side of life – what we have previously called pests, weeds or a mess – and it is revaluing that enables the forest gardener to support nature's transformational magic. And this goes much more than skin deep. It is much more than a mere acknowledgement that *all* creatures are important to a forest garden ecosystem.

When the human is no longer in charge, the forest garden is wide open to whosoever will come to visit or live there or die there: to eat or be eaten, to pollinate flowers, transfer seeds or eat them; to lay eggs, to be born and so on. Revaluing is a profound rearrangement of one's former opinions on the use or benefit, the harm or damage that you associate with particular creatures. It is about according everything you encounter in the forest garden recognition of its own inherent worth – just as it is, right there, right now. Within this complexity all of life is vital, the fly no less than the bee, the aphid no less than the butterfly.

When I began forest gardening I set out to grow only the perennial vegetables and other supporting plants that would (or were likely to) thrive in it, so that there was no need to make amendments to the soil or to offer special protection from the weather, etc. The motivation for that was to make my life easier. In time I learned that co-creating my garden with the natural world requires a deep acceptance of which plants are at home here. This springs from a different attitude that values and honours the uniqueness of this place, and which in turn enables the garden to integrate more fully into the local ecosystem and helps to support that system outside its boundaries.

revaluing me

In my early drafts of this chapter I wrote: "From the very outset I have placed great value on my own time and energy! I don't have enough of either and I never waste them with unnecessary work." Now I can see that previously I was completely missing the point and it has taken a long time for the true point to dawn on me and for me to realistically revalue myself. Yes, certainly my time and energy are valuable *to me*, however they are clearly not particularly important to the garden. If I were to be away or just not do anything in the garden for a year it would still be in much, much better shape than if all the spiders or beetles or bees were missing for a single season. There is simply no comparison or competition in my value relative to theirs.

It is humbling to recognise that you cannot begin to fathom the mystery and measure of the complex inter-relationships that exist and will exist in the forest garden, and because of this you know that any interventions you make are likely to destroy some beneficial relationships, as well as hopefully to foster others. It is far better to be deeply careful and respectful in your interactions with this precious place. What was previously seen as ordinary – not special or interesting in any way, and actually rather dull – has become special; so special that, at times, it might also be called sacred.

demonstrate appreciation

So once again the forest gardener pauses. This time it is in recognition of something even more special, the sense of the sacred. Appreciation is so much more than a thank you. It goes far, far deeper than that. Perhaps we humans have for so long regarded the world as our property, we have come to believe we are entitled to take what we need (or what we want). It is the polyculture mind and the polyculture heart that recognise that everything we have – and are – comes from the natural world, and that we are in receipt of priceless gifts that we have not earned, nor ever could. This profound reconfiguration of the forest gardener's values is perhaps best summed up or evidenced by this chapter's principle: demonstrate appreciation in meaningful and tangible ways. This is often a challenge, but once again there are no rules – we are all different, and will all find our different ways with this.

beauty and joy

We all recognise and appreciate beauty, and to live apart from it is to lose something very precious and to become distanced from life. Beauty is a part of the integrated whole and I think that perhaps it has its own essence that is instantly recognisable, heartfelt, moving and inspirational. To rejoice in simple, uncontrived beauty is an impetus towards deepening appreciation.

In my days as a conventional gardener I used to try to make my various gardens attractive. I never aimed as high as lovely or beautiful – just passably pleasant was my highest aspiration. Giving up control in a forest garden also means giving up attempting to contrive a particular aesthetic outcome. It had to not matter what the garden actually looked like – that was no longer the point, and by allowing the garden to take its own course a different beauty shone through.

> **A burdock plant grows up through a mass of parsley or wild marjoram. I do nothing; I watch and wait.**

Parsley and wild marjoram have been allowed to grow where they will. Burdock too has been able to seed itself anywhere it wishes. Some young burdock plants appear, growing through the already established parsley and marjoram plants and the result is beautiful and like a no-work harvest, this is no-work loveliness!

Edible plants everywhere, giving abundant harvests – that was what I wished for in my earliest forest garden dreams. I had not expected or anticipated the beauty that they would also bring and the joy that would inspire. How can it be that by giving no thought or planning to the aesthetic appeal of the garden, by letting nature do its own thing, by tossing pulled up plants, leaves and grass cuttings into piles and leaving them there – how is it that the end result is a far more

Burdock flowering through flat-leaved parsley

beautiful garden than I ever had before and one that contains many more beautiful aspects than I have ever seen anywhere?

But perhaps it is not really surprising at all that, by allowing the garden the freedom to express itself, I receive so much more beauty as it graciously reciprocates my endeavours to relinquish control. There is the joy of self-sown flowers, plants living out their natural cycles, unexpected combinations of flowers generated by nature which have somehow grown into beautiful combinations. And despite the sometimes challenging aesthetics of plants used as mulch and wild plants in the garden, it is beautiful, especially in summer when it is a veritable rhapsody of flowers.

eating with delight

In a conventional garden the gardener works and then reaps their rewards, and the harvest belongs solely to them. In the forest garden the harvest is shared and the gardener harvests *only enough*. They can joyfully and freely take their appropriate share and eating from the forest garden becomes an expression of the gardener's deep and fundamental connection with it.

Therefore, eat from your forest garden with joy and delight, with reverence, respect and awe, taking nothing for granted. Know that all the food grown there is a gift; one you have nurtured or smoothed the way for perhaps, but one that originates from far beyond you. Savour every mouthful and the special fragrances, the subtleties of taste and the visual delights that are particular to your own harvest – pungent garlic, crunchy apples, tart and juicy berries, hot onions, fresh dark greens, delightfully earthy roots, fragrant herbs. And then share these joys with family and friends – take them a basket or bowl of food, prepare and share a meal, give away plants, bulbs and seeds, cut bunches of flowers for friends, share skills, knowledge and understanding.

reciprocity

I am in France on a camping holiday. My partner and I are relaxing in the late afternoon sun and it is time to tidy up. Usually I take the coffee pot we use at home and give what is left to the garden. But this is a campsite, it is ordered and tidy, it is not my space and it doesn't feel right to empty the coffee filter we use on holiday on to the ground. But I now feel caught in a dilemma. I *always* give the coffee back to the Earth and I want to do that; it feels wrong not to. I realise that although this began as a functional thing, not to waste the nutrients in the coffee and not to clog up our plumbing, now it is deeper. I feel bound to the Earth, connected and in a sense obligated, and returning the coffee grounds takes on a different meaning – one of reciprocal giving back in a heartfelt way. I realise at this point that it has become a token of a different relationship, that it is symbolic, an offering and could also be described as a sacred act. I take the filter paper and the coffee grounds and gently place them under the shrubs just beyond our pitch at the edge of the campsite where they are out of sight and could just decompose in their own time without upsetting anyone. Since that day, when I empty the coffee pot, I do so consciously with respect and reverence.

Revaluing is happening from the very beginning of the forest garden journey and will never end. I think that all my early glimpses of appreciation were embedded in the wordless wonder of pausing, of waiting and of watching with polyculture eyes and that it is in following the polyculture path to the heart of the garden and becoming a different gardener that appreciation is most surely demonstrated.

the polyculture path to the heart of the garden

My 'garden of equal delights' was the place that demonstrated to me that nature is a source of true wisdom and that by quieting down and listening I can hear its gentle whispers and sense its subtle guidance

principle 11

Polyculture learning is slow learning

polyculture learning

A forest gardener is a different gardener but we all start off as conventional gardeners and this journey is one of profound change. Polyculture learning is the key to this change. It is not, emphatically not, about knowledge or certainty; rather it is about learning from experience, trusting, letting go of the old and embracing the new. There can be no haste in this, it is a work for life and what you need most is open polyculture eyes, an open polyculture mind and an open polyculture heart.

the old conventional gardener

I have always loved gardening and for over thirty years I was a very conventional gardener. I had six gardens over those years in the different places that I lived and whilst they were nothing special to anyone else they were my personal refuge and my delight. They had all the usual parts – lawns, shrubs and flower beds and all the usual flowers. I did all the usual gardening tasks, I weeded, I watered, I made compost and when the bin overflowed I took the excess greenery to the local recycling centre. I avoided the use of chemicals – that is apart from slug pellets which I used occasionally, but not regularly.

However, I was always secretly envious of people with 'better' gardens than me; but as much as I loved my garden I never had the time or energy or, for that matter, the necessary vision and skills to do it any differently. I had little understanding of plants and if I saw something I liked I expected it to grow and look good and was often disappointed when that didn't happen. I had often yearned to grow food but only actually made a few sporadic attempts. For a while I had an allotment at the same time as having young children but even getting there was nearly impossible! Needless to say it didn't turn out well. Once or twice since then I tried to grow tomatoes in pots as some friends do, but I was never able to emulate their success.

I watched gardening programmes on television and occasionally read a gardening magazine – or more likely just looked at the pictures. I was interested but not fascinated and certainly not obsessed!

a different gardener

But it is surprising sometimes, how change happens. Of course, it is always happening imperceptibly, whether we see it or not, but sometimes it comes right out of the blue, which is what happened to me. I certainly could never have foreseen becoming a radically different gardener with such a different garden, but discovering forest gardening divides my life into before and after, just like having children or finding your life partner. The two parts are so different but you don't know why or how until you experience it.

Before polyculture learning there comes conventional learning about forest gardens, starting with the theoretical background and then learning about the trees and plants that you hope to grow – their size and life span; their role(s) in an ecosystem; their temperature, soil, moisture and light requirements and how to grow and propagate them. This alone is a lot to take on board, but there is no hurry.

The forest gardener needs to start with this information, but the real, in-depth learning comes from experience – and time. Because we are freed from a good deal of labour, forest gardeners can spend time with the garden getting to know it in a different way, learning to support it gently with a light touch that we would never have thought possible before. The embryonic polyculture mind knows the vision that the heart is bearing, and it understands that freedom is vital to the emerging forest garden and is willing to revalue what happens in experience and to learn from it.

But, like an ecosystem, a forest gardener takes time to form. This is a gentle journey wherein polyculture learning leads us slowly into new ways of perceiving and relating to the garden. As forest gardeners, we learn slowly without realising that we are learning at all as we watch with polyculture eyes. In time we will know things and have fragments of insight and be able to trace their origins back to that watching and waiting and seeing. Doing nothing and letting the garden just *be* teaches us what we are ready to learn, as we develop our own polyculture mind. The polyculture mind develops the ability to interpret and interact with the garden as a whole system. It happens gradually as it silently rearranges our understanding of what a forest garden is, what or who it is for and how it works.

There is much challenge and change. The experience of exchanging places from the apex of a hierarchical pyramid of control for an interlinked place in a network of mutual support and co-operation will be far more taxing than any amount of book learning. The forest gardener finds over and over again that the human trait of dominance is challenged repeatedly and eventually we have an entirely different perception of the garden and of ourselves within the garden. We have become a different gardener and we have a polyculture heart.

the polyculture path

As you have no doubt gathered by now, I use polyculture as a metaphor to describe my experience in the forest garden. Derived from the multiplicity of plants that work together to comprise an ecological guild within a forest garden, I have always liked the way this word indicates multiple entities working together as one. Polycultures are the way I think, the way I relate and the way I connect to my garden.

First of all, I wanted a forest garden because I wanted a bargain with nature or perhaps from nature – more produce for less work – in the form of a productive and beautiful but low maintenance perennial garden. Later on, I found that crucially forest gardening is a radical move away from everything being for the benefit of people. The forest gardener gives up control and enters into a co-operative interactivity between many very different but equal beings, and nature plays a full role. However, human nature being what it is, I do think that wanting a 'bargain' will often be the starting point of this journey. What really matters is the attitude of mind and heart that the forest gardener develops as time goes by.

I realise now that I have been on a journey of profound change; change in the way I see my garden and the wider world, change in my values, intentions and inner self. These changes were *completely unexpected* at the outset. In an earlier draft of this chapter I wrote that they are at least as significant as the edible harvests, but now I must emphasise that, although the edible harvests are wonderful and very much appreciated, the personal, internal changes evoked on this journey are many times more significant. You can only eat an apple or a bowl of raspberries once, but positive personal change is enduring. This has been a journey of healing and re-integration and is a journey that will continue always. The forest garden and the forest gardener make the journey together. The garden knew all along where it was going; the gardener learned as she went along.

horticulture and accepted wisdoms

Conventional gardens, grown for both food and for their beauty, operate according to the practices of horticulture – this is the accepted wisdom, passed down through the generations. Practice has been modified over time by plant breeding, new techniques and so forth, but it has always provided a bedrock of knowledge and guidance to follow. The historic roots of horticulture lie in peasant holdings and cottage gardens and also in the ornate gardens of the aristocratic and the wealthy. In deference to this heritage, gardens are generally meant to be tidy and ordered. Currently there is a trend towards emulating the wilder side of gardens (which is especially noticeable at the large horticultural shows), but whilst this is in part recognition of the fact that nature is actually vital to the health of any garden, it does not spring from a deeper understanding that would truly allow the wild into the garden. But it is a start.

In conventional gardens the emphasis is on management, planning and control and the gardener's dominance rather than on ecology. Nature is distorted, packaged, parcelled and potted. It is fed with chemicals not nutrients, producing large overbred flowers, fruits and vegetables that can no longer reproduce themselves and that are very susceptible to disease. In terms of home-scale food growing, our conventional use of vegetable patches and allotments is an exercise in plant apartheid, with everything ranked in regimented rows of sameness. And in the flower garden what we have until now accepted as normal and indeed beautiful, may come to seem grotesque to us eventually.

Plants may be persuaded (forced) to live in surroundings they are not at home in, changing soil pH or other conditions in the attempt to make the garden conform to the gardener's plans rather than using what is at hand and what is suited to the locality. They are subjected to a utilitarian view of the world that exercises control to achieve its ends. In contrast, to stop controlling and start trusting nature is a very significant change of mind and heart.

The accepted wisdoms of weeding, pest management, digging and dead-heading have been shown to be detrimental to a forest garden that is developing as an ecosystem. The forest gardener learns that nature itself will provide all the benefits that these horticultural activities are intended to bring about.

To the outsider, forest gardeners with their polyculture eyes and polyculture mind spend a lot of time looking at nothing much and doing very little, whilst others toil in their gardens, bemoaning the amount of work involved, however much they actually enjoy what they do. The polyculture-minded gardener sits, watches and waits in increasingly joyous anticipation of ever-changing delights.

Participating with nature in the growth and development of the forest garden is not an easy transition to make; it is challenging, uncomfortable and can bring out all sorts of insecurities and fears. Leaving behind the attitudes and beliefs that we have all been immersed in all our lives is at once very simple and very difficult. It is simple to understand and in the context of forest garden theory it makes perfect sense. But it is harder to put into practice because it is the antithesis of how we humans see our place and function in the world. We believe that we are here to dominate and to control, not to stand aside and watch nature take over. But stand aside the forest gardener must. The changes engendered on the journey of becoming a forest gardener so fundamentally alter the relationship between the gardener and the natural world that they are significant enough to be described as a new paradigm.

relationship

If it is not control, what is the nature of the relationship we have entered into with our forest garden?

I have described the pause and shown how, during the pause, the forest gardener waits and watches, watches and waits and begins to learn patience. This pause in fact continues into the eternal and unforeseeable future because *this relationship with the garden is primarily pause.*

This new relationship is low key, less strident, kinder, calmer, more accepting altogether. It is about becoming aware of what makes the forest garden tick. Forest gardeners can never know the intricacies of how the garden's ecosystem actually works, but we are in awe of its deep and beautiful complexity. Refraining from automatic activity, and always seeking ways to promote the health and wellbeing of the garden is to love the garden for its own sake. In return the garden nurtures and nourishes the gardener in body and soul with food and with beauty. This is a relationship of equals, a familial and loving relationship.

The actual relationship began at first planting and, as in every relationship, trust is central to this one. Pausing, waiting and watching initiate the relationship; the very first pause was the indicator that the forest gardener was willing to trust. Watching and waiting, doing the minimum deepens trust further. As we adapt, adjust and alter our internal understandings and frames of reference, holding what we have always known in abeyance, new knowledge forms itself in our minds and hearts.

Nature has plenty to say about the evolution of this garden, as helpers from nearby visit or stay and play their own unique and vital parts. As time goes on and ever more plants, animals, insects and fungi arrive in the garden, the forest gardener learns the significance of strengthened ecological links with the neighbourhood, and learns about polyfloral polycultures and about nature's transformational magic. All of this learning is made possible by, and also builds, relationship.

Everything the gardener does and does not do, and every response from the forest garden to those actions and non-actions, as well as every spontaneous happening – all of these are aspects of this relationship. But this is to greatly simplify things, as in forest gardens there are hundreds, or even thousands, of active participants: the gardener, the piece of land that comprises the garden and every other plant, fungus and creature that lives in, on or under that piece of ground, and every creature that visits it.

As time goes by, the forest gardener becomes more adept at learning the language of their garden and how to converse – how both the individual plants and the forest garden ecosystem as a whole replies. The forest garden is constantly changing, which means that engaging with it is not a matter of always repeating what worked before (or for that matter what didn't work), it is always about interacting *now*.

There is no need to over-complicate or over-rationalise this, but just to trust and accept the outcome. This is a dance with nature. Follow the garden. There are no specific answers. I did not follow a formula with prescribed rules, but I tracked my way along the highways and byways of an unclear and somewhat shaded path; and as I travelled,

I fell in love with the garden differently. Or you could say I fell in love with a different garden. Not a garden for me and what I want, but a garden for all beings, a delightful garden. Equally delightful.

The tables have truly been turned. The gardener no longer dictates what must happen in this forest garden – the crops, the anticipated yields, the lengths we will go to in order to get what we want. Forest gardening has turned the human experience of being in control on its head. The forest gardener dreamed this garden, planned and planted it, all the while knowing that this was actually nature's garden. And as we pause, watch and wait, nature replies and takes up where we left off.

The control we consistently impose on the world around us and its other inhabitants, the disturbance and destruction that we entrain – these have all stopped. Instead, disturbance of another kind is visited on the forest gardener. This is inevitable. The whole experience goes against the grain of our culture and upbringing, our habitual patterns of behaviour. Learning to let nature take the lead is an alien concept and one that requires persistence and determination to stick to. It may in time become somewhat easier – more natural – but it will always be challenging. Perhaps future generations, if they start from a different place and experience, may be able to adhere to nature more faithfully, may be able to discern its moves more clearly, may just 'get it' in a way we cannot. But here is where we are and it is where we begin.

polyculture mind

A polyculture mind is the mind of this new paradigm where the former truths no longer apply. It understands and appreciates how biodiversity and biomass create health, fertility and abundance. It watches and waits with almost infinite patience and it learns slowly as it gains an intimate knowledge of the garden as a whole. It supports the forest gardener to do only the minimum. It is enraptured with more and more polyfloral polycultures, it sees life cycling though the garden, and nature's transformational magic weaving the whole ecosystem together.

Polyculture mind has learned this and more that cannot readily be captured in words. These learnings are a patchwork of intuited or otherwise sensed knowing which are woven into a deepening respect for and understanding of the garden. This is different to anything known previously and is much more than the sum of its parts. And so the forest gardener learns to slip into or beneath the skin of the garden and dance with the vibrant, delicate and yet robust cycles of growth and decay, as life weaves and re-weaves itself through the garden.

As experience grows, polyculture mind can also see how drastically we have cut ourselves off from nature, left its ways of seeing, being and doing and replaced them with our own. Consequently, we are left out of the bigger picture and we have unmet needs; we are separate, alone, unconnected and adrift. We have placed ourselves outside of the living systems of the planet. In the new forest gardening paradigm we are connected and nourished; we are provided for and as former meanings and interpretations are uprooted we find new meanings in the events unfolding in the garden. Polyculture mind understands the complexity and diversity of the garden and can apply the principles more wisely with a polyculture heart.

polyculture heart

All along it was polyculture heart that supplied abundant patience and was willing to wait, to watch, to listen and to learn; to co-create. Such passivity in a world of busy-ness and activity! But polyculture heart was born at that moment when control was surrendered to nature and then strengthened at every subsequent opportunity to reject control. Polyculture heart supplied trust too – in both the desire and the ability to trust in nature. At first this had to be a chosen intellectual position, but over time polyculture heart patiently held the vision when understanding foundered or was limited, in times of frustration and even apparent failure. Polyculture heart guided the forest gardener towards trust and lent wisdom to polyculture mind to discern a new way of being with the garden, learning from a place of innocence and simplicity.

Polyculture heart has learned to harvest and to enjoy whilst remembering to take only enough, leaving some behind for other creatures to enjoy with no regrets, and it bows in homage to all plants. From this deep caring for the garden springs heartfelt love, wonderment, deep appreciation, respect and reverence. There is great joy in nature's beauty and her gifts, there is trust and connection. There is humility too, a developing intuition and the sense that the forest garden has increasingly absorbed the forest gardener into itself.

The polyculture heart weighs things differently, revalues, has new insights. It cares differently because the balance has changed. A different equality is sought in the wider world and all other creatures matter much, much more than they ever did. There are new perspectives that call into question some of the most commonplace assumptions and attitudes about the non-human world. Human significance diminishes and diminishes again.

healing

Since its inception my garden of equal delights has grown exponentially. It has incorporated increasing numbers of resident animals from the plainly visible to the microscopic. It has become a healthy, vibrant and fertile mini ecosystem, but importantly it is also connected to the wider ecosystems beyond its boundaries. Strengthening the ecological links between the forest garden and the wider world beyond, means that many creatures that do not live there, will now nevertheless live because of it. There is beauty a-plenty, fertility and fruitful abundance. Lifecycles are repeated year after year: this is a resilient and enduring place. I have year-round fresh and healthy food, and although my spirit may be worn down at times, here in the garden I am at home and at peace.

To plant and tend a forest garden is to heal and repair our ruptured relationship with our planet. It is about coming home, getting grounded and answering what the land wants of the gardener. Bringing scattered and lost parts back together and reuniting them. In my garden this is about loving everything that lives without any discrimination – everything.

We have found our role, our niche in this place; and it is emphatically not that of the controller sitting atop a pyramid, being served and serviced by the life beneath us. Previously we were alienated from the ecosystem and joined to the rest of the human race in their strenuous efforts to force life into a dysfunctional alignment in which people dictate all the terms and conditions. But that attempt cannot last forever – because we are not so slowly strangling and poisoning that life out of existence. In an aligned and distributive world the opposite occurs and this is what the forest garden is for – to help us to find our own niche that truly works within the natural world. It is both to heal and to integrate.

Heart and healing is what the forest garden was about all along. I don't think it could have been otherwise once its purpose was no longer to fulfil my own personal wants. Healing is *implicit* from the outset in the cessation of control and all that follows naturally from that non action. It will become *explicit* one day when the forest gardener's polyculture heart understands the deeper purpose they have been drawn into.

the wholehearted declaration of peace

Life is at home in the forest garden and it has become a place of healing. *This healing lies in the gardener having wholeheartedly declared peace.* No longer does nature have to struggle against an alien controller, but it can just be in harmony with a deeply empathetic and understanding gardener. The old ways of control were a form of hatred and of violence, they were always frustrating and destructive but particularly to vulnerable and fragile and damaged ecosystems. The forest gardener can see nature healing in overgrown places and its wild weeds as its sign of forgiveness.

Formerly the threads of nature were as fine filaments blowing in the wind, fragile and easily torn apart. Here they have been re-woven into a stronger and more resilient fabric and this place is being healed. Importantly the support offered by the forest gardener has facilitated and speeded that healing. But they must beware lest they start to let any of the fine threads detach themselves once again and begin to unravel this healing. Enlightened and gentle support for the garden may be vital for generations yet to come to more fully repair the havoc that has been wrought thus far. Our joint debt to repay is not to save the world for our own sakes but to help to heal it for its own.

> *Integrity is wholeness, the greatest beauty is organic wholeness, the wholeness of life and things, the divine beauty of the universe. Love that, not man apart from that ...*
>
> ~ Robinson Jeffers, from *The Answer*, 1936

polyculture being

In the forest garden, life leads and polyculture eyes, mind and heart follow. Everything flows from this interaction. The forest gardener is becoming an integral part of the garden, not through conscious choice, wish or desire but simply by spending time, absorbing themselves in the garden as an integral part of a single living entity. The view from the inside is absolutely the reverse of the view they once had from outside. The gardener starts to see, or think about seeing, as though from the point of view of the garden's many inhabitants – the moths, spiders, fungi, aphids, slugs, hedgehogs, birds, spiders, beetles, worms, bees and all the rest of the extended family.

Slowly, slowly a more complex, but never quite complete picture emerges, and it becomes clearer that this garden is a single entity, a united whole. Before we perceived ourselves to be superior beings, but now we have shifted towards recognising a parity between all creatures. The balance between power and control and freedom is shifting. Impulses to control continue to arise – the cultural conditioning is strong – and sometimes they are acted out, but hopefully less frequently. At least control is now seen for what it is and always was – distance and separation from nature, feeling set apart, acting aloof and superior. The folly of all that is known, recognised and laughed at.

The former need to be the sole beneficiary of the forest garden has become irrelevant. This garden is for all of nature and every creature and plant that can find a niche here and live out their life cycle. Produce for the forest gardener is still important but this is very far from being the main purpose. Something fundamental has shifted and will not, ever, shift back – the forest gardener passed the point of no return a long time ago. The welfare, wellbeing, vitality and integrity of the whole garden has become far more important than that of any individual member of its community. Individuals may need and receive support, nurturing and attention but nobody is intrinsically more important than anybody else.

Forest gardening begins with the intention of gardening in nature's own image. At the outset, these are merely words and we do not know what it is that we are actually embarking on. However, in time, after a great deal of slow polycultural learning, the forest gardener sees differently with polyculture eyes, thinks differently with a polyculture mind and acts differently with a polyculture heart. By this time the forest gardener has become a truly polycultural being. We have found our own specific niche in the forest garden and also in nature beyond its boundaries. It is in our heart and in our blood. We have moved from identifying with nature to identifying as nature, to becoming an integral part of nature, so that the actions of forest garden and forest gardener are as one. We know this and maybe the community of all living beings recognises these profound changes within that have led us to becoming one with the Earth community.

apprentice

Here I am in my forest garden and the realisation dawns that there is a deep and profoundly simple sacred aspect to the wisdom of nature flowing through the forest garden. I have done little but make space for nature; and in stark contrast to my conditioned belief system that I need to work hard to obtain food, it is feeding me. Compared to my former conventional self I am doing almost nothing, I have my bargain, but it is a very different bargain to the one I imagined.

The point of actualising a deeper integration into nature is not wanting to take, take, take, not even to give and take reciprocally, but to give and give; yes with some taking – but only just enough if we can be humble enough for this. The polyculture heart is not greedy. The forest garden gives gifts (harvests) to us, and all of the ecology in the garden, equally according to need. We, as part of an equalising or distributive ecology, give back our part by our life-centred actions and non-actions. We give nurture, we give love.

We are but one of the creatures sitting at nature's banqueting table and we have no intrinsically greater claim on the goodness and productivity of the natural world than any of the other creatures who also live here. Like them, we can legitimately and lovingly use plants for our true needs for food and fuel, for artefacts and accessories to living, but in proportion, naturally, in balance and never to excess.

The younger we can start to un-learn the ways of control and begin to tread the polyculture path, the better. Our children and grandchildren are crucial to the future and will be here when we are not, and they will take on the guardianship of their places. It is important to teach them while they are young and can learn with ease what they would soon learn to question.

Our own grandchildren love to visit and to spend time in the garden. I was weaving sticks from the hedge round a polyculture bed to make an edge when Amber and Luke spontaneously picked up some of the sticks on the ground and enthusiastically joined in. One-year-old Amelie sat motionless and entranced in the sunshine as she watched the 'busy-bees' on the 'mimigolds' in our first forest garden. Then she pulled a leaf from a plant and just dropped it to the ground – clearly she had seen me doing the same! Two-year-old Pip held my hand and walked round the garden fascinated by the swelling apples, plums and pears. She ate red, white and blackcurrants and raspberries straight from the bushes, she munched small runner beans raw, and as for the Japanese wineberries ... she had the lot! Emmi will be walking soon and exploring what the garden holds for her.

The forest gardener has all along been nature's own direct apprentice. We have learned directly and authentically from nature, from life. Unmediated and unimpeded by the bias inherent in us from our earliest days, we have learned to trust our own understanding of nature expressing itself in the forest garden. This knowledge means that we can step aside from absolute truths and rights and wrongs, to the relative and the subjective; context and meaning become all important.

This is certainly not controlling nature and neither is it working with nature as if it were on a more or less 50/50 basis, though once upon a time that was a radical enough idea. As a forest gardener I recognise my own rapidly diminishing significance. In my days of horticultural gardening the actual balance of power was 100/0 – the garden had no say in the decisions being made. On becoming a forest gardener the balance slowly slid down through 50/50, 30/70 to 10/90 and lower still, reducing all the time towards a more appropriate assessment of my own importance. Where does it finally come to a halt? Perhaps at 1/99? Or 0.1/99.9? I don't know. This is the magic journey of discovery – how small, how diminutive can I become within this system, this family, this place and yet still experience its abundance? Ultimately neither I nor you are the gardener. Life is the gardener.

Our polyculture eyes and ears and skin sense the outer world and draw it into the inner world. Our polyculture mind is the mind of the seasons, the wind and the rain, the mud and snow, ice and sun. Mind of bee, bird and worm; mind of connection, interconnection and inter-dependence. Our polyculture heart loves and appreciates all this simply but deeply. Our attitude is of humble respect and reverence. And we know without a shadow of doubt that our place in this world is beside the apple tree, the kale and the onions, the daisy and dandelion and the nettle, alongside the birds and worms and butterflies – and everything else that cannot be named here. One with them all, we need to welcome the wild.

welcome the wild

*Now is the unfolding of forever and as all the trees and
plants in the forest garden live out their own life cycles,
generation upon generation, life itself cycles
through the garden.*

principle 12

Welcome the wild

This life cycling through the garden in ever increasing circles is the
wild – and forest gardening means welcoming the wild. Life is wild
and the wild is life. Wildness is essential and the journey of forest
gardening is a return (home) to the wild.

We have dissected the wild and invented various conceptual
pigeonholes to put the parts we created into. There is the pigeonhole
for tame and domesticated animals and plants that are useful to us,
there is another one for the intriguing, attractive and cute wildlife
we encourage into our gardens or go outside to look for, and yet
another for the difficult or scary wildlife we would rather never see.

We think and act as though we are different to the wild, better than
it probably; that we are civilised and we have tamed the planet and
our human environment, and domesticated animals and plants. We
have re-made the world in an image we prefer, where we like to
think we are in control. But, however much we surround ourselves
with artefacts of our own construction and design (living or
otherwise), we are not separate and never can be. So where is the
wild?

The wild is away from here, far away, or so we think. We may think
that we rarely encounter the wild, and certainly I have never seen a
wild tiger or elephant or shark or polar bear or any other exotic wild
animal in their natural habitat. But I have seen a worm. There are no

tame worms. There are no tame spiders or blackbirds, or frogs, beetles and hedgehogs. Although some of their cousins are caged animals in zoos and parks and also laboratories of course.

The wild is everywhere... in the soil, in the air, the wind, the rain, in the water, in every being in the garden. The wild is in weather, in the cold frosty, freezing blizzards of winter, in the torrents of rain turning the ground to a mud bath and flooding homes and businesses, in the gales blowing trees over. This weather we can easily recognise as wild, but equally wild is the mild warmth of spring, the full-bodied hug of summer and in the clear and mellow autumn days. It may be more apparent sometimes than others but the weather is always wild and is always determining our welfare.

We cannot survive without everything the wild is and does. We may be able to artificially fertilise soil (to some extent) but when it comes to the crunch we cannot do without the activity of all the wild worms and wild bacteria, fungi, protozoa and everything else wild in the soil. We may be able to irrigate land, but we cannot do it without the wild streams and rivers bearing wild rain on its way to the wild seas. We cannot do without the wild bees (as well as the domesticated honeybees) or without the wild eaters of carrion and other detritus. We need wild plants, we need wild trees, we need everything wild and we need to see the wild as life arriving in its own time, renewing, restoring, healing.

In that prolonged pause, the forest gardener begins to let the wild into their understanding. A wild understanding rejects the horticultural apartheid that reckons domesticated plants good and wild plants bad, and the dominion over life that destroys rather than heals. Whilst watching and waiting, the forest gardener relinquishes the control that segregates plants into single monocultural rows, the control that destroys the natural systems and thereby damages and degrades the soil, reduces fertility, wrecks biodiversity and encourages the pests and diseases that it sought to control in the first place. In ceasing to control, the forest gardener lets the wild back into the garden. 'Who will speak for us?' say the worms, the birds, caterpillars, the spiders and the mice, the ants, beetles and rabbits. And the forest gardener answers, 'I will'.

When nature moves in to repair and restore the harm we caused, we habitually grumble at it for doing so. But forest gardeners have learned that we need nature to heal over our scars and we have given up trying to persecute it out of existence. Instead we recognise the value of the wild returning to the garden as the ecosystem develops and matures, because biologically and accountably we are all of one piece with all wild things and with life. The same air flows in our lungs, the same water hydrates us, we eat other beings and our wastes ultimately feedback to other creatures. We have envisioned ourselves as separate, special, different, but we are not. We are not more and we are not less than other beings. We are the same and we must find the humility to admit it and to live from it. We need to welcome the wild, wholeheartedly, and to be at peace with it.

Previously I explained the way a forest garden generates its own fertility, health and abundance and all the principles of forest gardening directly relate back to this concept of the ecosystem. But it is just a concept – a way of explaining things so we can try to understand. However, an ecosystem is not a 'thing' in the way that my house or my shoes are things. And in the end an ecosystem is simply a human construct – just another tame word for the wild. The wild is what sustains and enables the ecosystem.

The wild is there in polyfloral polycultures and in life-cycle gardening; it is certainly the essence of supporting nature's transformational magic and harvesting only enough. In short, at every point of considering the forest garden and interacting with it, the wild has in fact been the predominant consideration. Forest gardeners too are wild – our integration into the forest garden has been an initiation into the wild and we are no longer 'tame', our own domesticity too is an illusion. Apart from a very few people living simply in the remotest parts of the globe, most of us don't have a clue about how to be wild. But once forest gardeners have recognised the sacredness of the garden, we are closer to the wild than ever before. And when we tread the polyculture path to the heart of the garden we are returning towards our own wilder self, towards our own home ground. The measure of the forest gardener is the measure of our comfortable integration into the wildness of the natural world where we live. We have moved from controlling and fighting the natural world to peace, from estrangement to coming home, from destruction to repair and regeneration, from separation towards unity and to a different way of understanding the default state of an uncorrupted, uncontrolled and undisturbed world. We sense a kinship with all other creatures on an increasingly equal basis and we have reverence for all of wild nature.

Blackbird pausing from eating ivy berries

welcoming the wild

I don't know why it took me so long to realise that we are not just surrounded by the wild, but that we are wild too and completely dependent on the wild. Perhaps because it is such a profoundly different way of looking out at the world. When the wild knocks at the boundaries of your garden asking to be allowed in, it will be life itself looking for a way in, seeking a crack or an opportunity through which to enter. And therefore all you need to do is to be open to that opportunity and see where it takes you. It will be the whole seeking its disparate parts, trying to breach the void, reunite and reintegrate them. Life is the gardener, and the forest gardener recognises that it is calling us to pay attention. This is a call to heal the land, heal the people and heal the rift between us. Perhaps it is why the wild keeps on coming back to find us.

gardening with life

*I've always wondered why people call plants wild. We don't
think of them that way. They just come up wherever they
are and like us they are at home in that place.*

~ Clara Jones Sargosa of the Chukchansi people

Forest gardening has brought benefits to my life that I never would
have thought possible. Where once there were lawn, hedges and a
few shrubs there are now hundreds of diverse plants and trees.
Before there was nothing for me to eat and precious little for visiting
wildlife either. Now my garden of equal delights is a place of edible
abundance providing tasty food all year round that requires very
little time or physical effort. It is often enchantingly lovely and at the
same time it is an ecological haven for more creatures than I could
ever recognise or name.

Forest gardening is about co-creating a different way forward
wherein easy abundance, health and healing are the new norms and
I no longer see this as particularly special or even unusual. It is life
taking care of itself and getting back to normal – or what was once
normal. What has passed as normal for too long is maladjusted,
forced, artificial, frail, manipulated, overdone, extreme, fanciful,
poisoned, useless in many respects, and dead or dying in many
places. In a forest garden we learn that the living world has its own
inherent completeness and integrity that is encoded in nature, and
can be accessed with polyculture eyes and mind. This is a pattern of
being that explains and unlocks how to be peaceful with a world,
where things work as they were meant to. Normal should be when
things work, when they function as nature intended, when we don't
have to resort to artificial means to do it for them because we have
previously prevented what is normal from working.

Because forest gardens embody and embed the natural world within
them, they invite us on a journey towards a different frame of

reference, different ways of being, seeing and doing. This is life extending itself and inviting us to meet with it and to collaborate and to co-create beautiful places. It is asking – maybe even pleading – that we put aside our dominance and the need to engineer outcomes, and learn to surrender to nature's infinite wisdom whilst we learn wisdom of our own. To become its apprentices whilst we grow into unity with it. This is the end of war with the garden, with nature, and with life and it is the beginning of peace. It is a journey that takes an open mind and transforms it into a polyculture mind, open eyes become polyculture eyes and an open heart becomes a polyculture heart – a connector of broken parts, a maker of wholes, a lover of beauty and a healer of places and people.

This is the ability to find a radically different relationship with nature, one that is not predicated solely on human needs or wants and which is not subject to human utilitarian values and the concomitant damage we inevitably inflict. It seeks an integration that is not a collision of the human world with the natural or wild world; but an integration that is about welcoming the wild, until you find that place of adaptation when there is no *wild* as such, there is just what there is. Such an integration is not new, however; it was the way of life for thousands of years.

traditional environmental knowledge

Prior to the European settlement and colonisation of other continents, countless individual tribes of indigenous peoples lived in a state of embedded harmony with their environment – and had done so for thousands of years. In her book about the indigenous peoples of California, *Tending the Wild,* M. Kat Anderson describes a place of almost mythic beauty and abundance. There was incredible diversity of natural ecosystems including floral meadows stretching for miles, prairies, woodlands and forests each with their own animal life. There were immense numbers of animals, birds and fish – bears, bighorn sheep, elk, antelope, mountain lions, wolves and the now extinct black jaguar. There were estimated to be tens of millions of resident and migratory birds and the rivers were burgeoning with fish, including millions of salmon.

However this was not, as the European settlers assumed at the time, a natural landscape, but one that had been incredibly sensitively and carefully tended and managed for centuries by the indigenous peoples. Their ability to work with nature to create and sustain enduring abundance was founded upon the deep, complex and enduring relationship between the people and their environment. They had vast knowledge about all aspects of the plant and animal worlds, they knew how to utilise their surroundings for food, housing, clothing, fuel, medicine and more. Anderson describes indigenous peoples' interaction with the natural world as one of immense complexity and sophistication wherein they increased the diversity and abundance of plants and animals; and whilst they used and disturbed their environment, they did not push it past the limits of regeneration. However their way of life and of tending the wild was so subtle as to be unrecognisable as such to the European settlers who arrived and dismissed native ways as inferior to their own agricultural practices.

Likewise 8,000 years ago in Central America the Mayan people, living in what is present day Guatemala, were growing ecologically sensitive and productive forest gardens. Today their marginalised descendants still practice an integrated agriculture, forestry and forest garden system that maintains fertility, high levels of biodiversity, manages water in the landscape and includes semi-domesticated animals. They need no fossil fuels and their land use practices store carbon in the soil for the long term.

becoming indigenous

The forest gardening journey could, I would suggest, be seen as a first step on the path to becoming indigenous people again. This is indigenous not in the sense of having always lived in a particular place, but in the sense of (now) belonging to that place. It is not about returning the land to some unknowable, pre-existing or assumed pristine state, but about re-learning how to make a life-long bond with a place, a bond that may one day be unbreakable.

My original motivation of a bargain, now long spent, would not have brought me here. The garden itself has brought me to this point. It taught me day by day by showing what it could do when left to its own innate wisdom and purpose. It showed me abundance, joy and delight and I learned the delicate dance of reciprocation. The garden revealed insights to polyculture eyes and mind. It showed polyculture heart the meaning and means of healing. It took me on and both integrated and rehabilitated me from a place of exclusion and control, to a place of peace.

It is not from ourselves that we will learn to be better than we are.

~ Wendell Berry ~

Although this forest garden journey is a profound change of heart and direction, I think it is just scratching the surface. Perhaps it will take generations of unlearning and new learning, and a great deal of humility, to come to a more appropriate and harmonious relationship with the Earth.

My take on forest gardening has always been on the wilder side. This has been deliberate because I wanted to push that particular boundary and find out what would happen, and clearly none of our growing landscapes would work without the wild elements both within and without their ecosystems. My small forest garden on a Welsh hillside fits into the larger ecology of the neighbouring gardens, farmland and woods by virtue of the many and varied insects, animals and birds that live and feed thereabouts. Uncontained by human boundaries they need a wider landscape to call home and to thrive in because in the actual 'real world' it is not possible to draw a line around any single area or ecosystem that distinguishes or separates it from another one; and life will be continually crossing any boundary we may arbitrarily draw. So, what happens or does not happen in my garden affects my neighbours' gardens, the woods across the road and the farms up and down the hill. And vice versa – what happens in those places affects my garden too. But further afield, across their farther boundaries, their ecologies are interacting with yet others – down in the valley, across to the river, amongst the distant hills or along the river and the canal to the town with its industrial estates and the nearby nature reserves, along the roadside verges and the railway line and eventually reaching the very different terrain of the mountains, the moors and the coast.

Where once there was a global, strong, resilient, functionally interconnected nest of ecosystems, today in so many places life is clinging on and hanging together by a thread. In many places those fine threads have already broken and much life has been lost. Because ecosystems are (at least potentially) everywhere, a forest garden opens up the possibility to connect with life, and to enhance, sustain and protect it as a whole even beyond the garden boundary, with small local ecosystems effectively nested within larger and yet larger ones, such that all life is connected and interdependent. Thus every part of every place is an important part of the whole, every link is needed; and when any connections break everything else is impacted.

Each place – whether small or large – that can become a functioning, healthy ecosystem can make a meaningful difference. Size is not significant. Everywhere is significant because it is an intrinsic and indispensable part of the whole. We have been warned for years about the decline in honeybee forage plants and more recently about huge declines in insect numbers more generally. Because the earth-wide losses are so huge, every little bit of respite and repair that nature can get is disproportionately valuable and can have more, not less, impact. The last animals and plants in any population are rightly deemed as supremely important. Why would we wait until we are down to the last remaining ants or dandelions to value them?

celebrate and support life

As an individual it can be hard and dispiriting to look for ways to make a real and significant difference to the problems of this world. But in our gardens, we can. In the UK alone there are 27 million households, an estimated 90% of which have a garden or outside space. Conventional, horticultural gardens stocked with the same garden centre staples are better than paved deserts, but they are not enough and they are not making the best of the space available. Converted to forest gardens there would be so much more to gain for both their people and the natural world.

Even in the tiniest of spaces afforded by contemporary housing developments it is possible to make positive changes by removing paving and patios, etc., clothing the fences and walls with climbers, planting native shrubs, polyfloral flowers and herbs and edible plants. A small fruit tree or large fruit bush, a perennial kale, some perennial onions and a collection of herbs will fit into the smallest of spaces and produce edible treats for much of the year, whilst providing some food and habitat for local insects and birds.

At the other end of the spectrum, many people have gardens that are larger than they either want or can manage. Let nature in more. I know there are aesthetic considerations but if it is out of sight and it really doesn't matter to anyone, let the hedges grow higher, let the wild plants in and just cut them off (or ask your gardener to do so) rather than pulling them up or digging them out. Let them decompose where they grew. Less work for you and more help for nature. If you have lots of space – maybe even acres – then grow a wood or, if that is too much work or too expensive (or both), then let nature do it for you.

Nor is this limited to forest gardening as based upon a woodland edge ecosystem. This is one model of what could be called an eco-systemic garden. Other gardens can be structured to fit into different ecologies – heath, meadow, moor, coast or bog and more. There are plenty of plants to choose for every habitat and circumstance – it is where they came from after all!

This then, is my hope for the future – the immediate future. Forest gardens – eco-systemic gardens – everywhere. Beautiful places, incorporating native and wild species, producing local food; and all based on the unique interaction of the individual gardener who is learning to integrate themselves within their own locality. And as we individually lovingly tend our own gardens of delight – each one significant in its own right – we can collectively transform ever larger areas into whole landscapes of edible and equal delight.

In this there would be no right or wrong – intention is everything. By the time a place becomes a site for a home and a garden it will have had many previous human uses – as land for agriculture or woods, previous development for housing or some other urban purpose for industry or civic purposes. We cannot hope to restore anything that might genuinely be an indigenous or natural land use, and our forest gardening may turn out to be an interim phase until we collectively learn or discern what the next steps may be. Right now we have a unique opportunity to heal our places, and also ourselves.

In writing this book my intention has been to set out straightforward principles that can provide guidance to forest gardeners, or ordinary gardeners, who seek to integrate themselves into the ecosystem of their garden. Each place is unique and each gardener is unique and it is the combination of place, person, purpose, perception and decisions that will create each unique forest garden. By pinning down what it means in each garden to do only the minimum, to plant polyfloral polycultures, to support nature's transformational magic and to harvest only enough... each forest gardener will discover for themselves what is and is not appropriate in their own patch. Thus my explanation of my inter-activity with my own garden is entirely personal and just one small example of what a forest garden can be. The scope for other outcomes, when different people and places interact with their own local ecologies, is infinite.

Forest gardening holds a key to the future. The polyculture path to the heart of the garden integrates us with the garden we have chosen to plant and all the wild elements within and around it. Any garden – forest garden or not – can be tended with the care and understanding learned in the forest garden, with the intention of creating a life supporting ecosystem and linking to the larger ecosystems beyond.

In addition to everything above, I would include all the personal changes experienced on the polyculture path to the heart of the garden as another vital aspect of the bigger picture. And when those changes are taken to heart by enough people there can potentially be social change as well.

What was it that whispered to me that summer afternoon when I first idly wondered if it might be possible to have a garden filled with perennial plants that were also edible? Where did that idea drop from? Why did it crystallise in my consciousness? Whatever was that compulsion I felt to find out more and to follow wherever it led? I can't say. Is it possible that, from the very beginning, life was in fact the instigator of all this (in me)? Writing it down makes it sound far-fetched but that's what it feels like. It would mean life was actively seeking wholeness, healing, unity.

Although I once saw myself as totally separate, I never really was – I was always simply one small part of nature's whole – I just didn't know it. Now I realise that I am but one creature among innumerable others, and although it is *my* garden, I have abrogated my human-centred 'right' to be in control. Life has its own processes by which one creature sustains another through complex streams of interdependence. I have been grafted into the garden as part of this magnificent complexity; I keep on watching and waiting and doing the minimum, and as far as possible I allow life to do its own thing. The crucial things are to relax and to trust. To relax not just for an interlude, not just in the pause as an initial rest from control, but to relax permanently. And to put our trust in nature – there are no half measures here – trust is trust with no holding back.

A forest gardener has planted themselves into their garden and also into life. I didn't fully realise what I meant when I concluded my previous book with this sentence. "We feel and we have become, closely linked with nature and her cycles and our own roots sink down deeper into life." I had an inkling then but now I know: because the forest gardener needs to see that ultimately life is the bigger picture – not just human life, but all life equally; the wholeness of life within which we are all embedded. Life links everything in the forest garden in a positively reinforcing cycle and it is life that flows through each of the principles in this book: life expressed in endless diversity, in flowers, in transformation from body to body and state to state and life paid homage and held sacred.

Life expressed in polycultures of place and polycultures of mind, eye and heart. Life loved, enhanced and protected. Life that creates more habitat, more diversity, more connections, more resilience. And more gardens of delight.

The garden is not just at my home – it is home – because it is where I find belonging. It is where I fit, where I belong and have purpose and meaning. Where I 'get' what is going on, the place I love above all other places, in my very own little niche, doing my own thing.

And so I invite you to a radically different relationship with the natural world as it manifests in your garden – an open door to inter-activity with nature and with life in an abundant edible garden. A garden that is healthy and fertile and – because you are not interfering and setting nature back – also far less demanding of what we know as 'work'. A place of beauty, of nourishment and refreshment; revitalising to people and to the myriad other creatures that live in it and visit it. The learnings you will experience are gifts from the garden and from life as you take your own place ever nearer to the heart of the garden. Love life. Garden with life.

appendix 1

trees and plants table

The trees, bushes, shrubs, perennials and other plants listed below have all grown in the garden of equal delights and the vast majority are still here. However as conditions have changed some of them have decided they no longer want to grow here but at least 200 different plants and trees are growing at the time of writing and no doubt there will be plenty more to come in the future.

Name	Benefits	Where
Fruit - trees		
Apple, Bramley	Edible, early blossom[7]	Polyculture beds
Apple, Ellison's Orange	Edible, early blossom	Edge bed
Apple, Falstaff	Edible, early blossom	Edge bed
Apple, Newton Wonder	Edible, early blossom	Polyculture beds
Apple, Sunset	Edible, early blossom	Polyculture beds
Apple, Trwyn Mochyn	Edible, early blossom	Polyculture beds
Cherry, Cariad	Edible, early blossom	Triangle bed
Cherry, Morello	Edible, early blossom	Long border
Cherry, Stella	Edible, early blossom	Polyculture beds
Damson, unknown variety	Hedging	Hedge
Gage, Cambridge	Edible, early blossom	Polyculture beds
Gage, Dennistons Superb	Edible, early blossom	Long border
Medlar	Edible, early blossom	Polyculture beds
Mirabelle, Ruby	Edible, early blossom	Long border
Pear, Catillac	Edible, early blossom	Edge bed
Pear, Concorde	Edible, early blossom	Long border
Pear, Invincible	Edible, early blossom	Long border
Pear, unknown	Edible, early blossom	Edge bed
Plum, Denbigh	Edible, early blossom	Polyculture beds
Plum, Marjorie's Seedling	Edible, early blossom	Polyculture beds
Plum, Victoria	Edible, early blossom	Polyculture beds

[7] I have used 'blossom' for plants that attract lots of insects and 'floral' for flowering plants that are less attractive to insects.

Name	Benefits	Where
Quince, *(Cydonia oblonga)*	Edible, early blossom	Long border
Quince, Vranja	Edible, early blossom	Long border
Fruit – bushes / plants		
Amelanchier	Edible, early blossom	Triangle bed, long border
Blackberry, thornless variety	Edible, early blossom	Hedge
Blackcurrant, 2 varieties	Edible, early blossom	Polyculture beds, triangle bed, long border
Blue sausage fruit, *(Decaisnea fargesii)*	Edible	Edge bed
Boysenberry	Edible, early blossom	Hedge
Cherry plum	Edible, early blossom	Hedge
Chocolate vine, *(Akebia quinata)*	Edible	Hedge
Elderberry, black	Edible, early blossom	Hedge
Elderberry, wild	Edible, early blossom	Hedge
Fig, Brown turkey	Edible, early blossom	Hedge
Goji berry	Edible	Hedge
Gooseberry, Hinomaki Red	Edible, early blossom	Long border, polyculture beds
Gooseberry, wild	Edible, early blossom	Hedge
Honeyberry, 2 varieties	Edible, early blossom	Polyculture beds
Japanese wineberry	Edible, early blossom	Edge bed
Jostaberry	Edible, early blossom	Long border, edge bed, polyculture beds
Kiwi fruit, 2 varieties	Edible	Hedge
Nanking Cherry	Edible	Polyculture beds
Nepalese raspberry	Edible	Polyculture beds
Raspberry, 3 varieties	Edible, early blossom	Edge bed, hedge
Raspberry, wild	Edible, early blossom	Long border
Redcurrant	Edible, early blossom	Long border, edge bed
Strawberry, 2 named varieties and wild plants	Edible	Polyculture beds
Whitecurrant	Edible, early blossom	Long border, edge bed
Edible greens - perennial		
Asparagus	Edible	Polyculture bed
Caucasian spinach	Edible	Edge bed
Good King Henry	Edible	Polyculture beds
Kale, Daubenton's	Edible	Polyculture beds
Kale, Taunton Deane	Edible	Polyculture beds
Kale, unknown variety (giant like)	Edible, blossom	Polyculture beds
Kale, variegated Daubenton's	Edible	Polyculture beds
Leaf beet	Edible	Edge bed

Name	Benefits	Where
Mountain sorrel	Edible	Polyculture beds
Pachyphragma microphyllum (edible brassica)	Edible, blossom	Polyculture beds
Sorrel	Edible	Polyculture beds
Turkish rocket	Edible, blossom	Long border
Wild rocket	Edible	Edge bed, long border
Edible greens – reseeding annuals		
Lamb's lettuce, large leaved	Edible, blossom	Polyculture beds, long border
Land cress	Edible, blossom	Polyculture beds, long border
Perennial root vegetables		
Chinese artichoke	Edible	Polyculture beds, triangle bed
Earth nut pea	Edible, blossom	Long border
Ground nut *(Apios americana)*	Edible roots, nitrogen fixer	Edge bed
Jerusalem artichoke, 2 varieties	Edible	Polyculture beds, long border, triangle bed
Mashua	Edible, blossom	Edge bed
Oca, 3 varieties	Edible	Polyculture beds, long border, triangle bed
Pig nut	Edible	Edge bed
Scorzonera	Edible, blossom	Long border, triangle bed
Skirret	Edible, blossom	Long border, polyculture beds
Reseeding root vegetables		
Japanese burdock	Edible, blossom	All areas
Salsify	Edible, blossom	All areas
Edible onions		
Chives	Edible, blossom	Polyculture beds, long border, edge bed
Few flowered leek	Edible, blossom	Long border, hedge, edge bed
Garlic 2 varieties	Edible	Long border, triangle bed, polyculture beds
Ornamental/edible alliums, 2 varieties	Edible, blossom	Polyculture beds, triangle bed
Perennial leek	Edible, blossom	Polyculture beds, triangle bed, long border
Three cornered leek	Edible, blossom	Long border, hedge, edge bed
Tree onion	Edible	Polyculture beds, long border

Name	Benefits	Where
Welsh onion	Edible, blossom	Polyculture beds
White onion, from greengrocer, planted	Edible, blossom	Polyculture beds
Wild garlic	Edible, blossom	Hedge, polyculture beds
Conventional annual vegetables		
Carrots	Edible, blossom	Long border
Field beans	Edible, blossom, nitrogen fixer	Long border
Parsnip	Edible, blossom	Long border, triangle bed
Peas	Edible, blossom, nitrogen fixer	Edge bed
Radish	Edible, blossom	Polyculture beds
Runner beans	Edible, blossom, nitrogen fixer	Polyculture beds, edge bed
Herbs		
Angelica	Edible, blossom	Triangle bed
Bay	Edible	Long border, triangle bed, hedge
Elecampane	Blossom	Triangle bed
Fennel	Edible, blossom	Polyculture beds, long border, edge bed, triangle bed
Feverfew	Blossom	Long border
Germander	Medicinal, blossom	Long border
Horseradish	Edible	Polyculture beds
Hyssop, 3 varieties	Medicinal, blossom	Long border, triangle bed
Lavender, 3 varieties	Edible, blossom	Polyculture beds, long border, triangle bed
Lemon balm	Edible, blossom	Polyculture beds, edge bed
Lovage	Edible, blossom	Polyculture beds
Marjoram, cultivated variety	Edible, blossom	Long border
Marjoram, wild	Edible, blossom	Long border, edge bed, polyculture beds
Mint, 4 varieties	Edible, blossom	Long border
Mullein	Blossom	Polyculture beds
Parsley	Edible, blossom	Triangle bed
Red-veined sorrel	Edible	Polyculture beds, long border, edge bed
Rosemary	Edible, blossom	Long border
Salad burnet	Edible	Polyculture beds
Sage	Edible, blossom	Long border

Name	Benefits	Where
Sweet cicely	Edible, blossom	Polyculture beds, long border, edge bed, triangle bed
Tansy	Blossom	Triangle bed
Thyme, 3 varieties	Edible, blossom	Long border, edge bed, polyculture beds
'Edimentals'		
Aquilegia	Edible flowers	Triangle bed
Bistort, 2 varieties	Edible leaves, blossom	Polyculture beds, edge bed
Calendula	Edible flowers, blossom	Long border
Cowslip	Edible flowers, blossom	Triangle bed
Day lily, 2 varieties	Edible flowers	Triangle bed
Dog tooth violet	Edible, blossom	Triangle bed, long border
Eleagnus, 2 varieties	Edible fruits, nitrogen fixer	Hedge, long border
Evening primrose	Edible roots, blossom	Triangle bed
Fuchsia, 3 varieties	Edible (fruits)	Edge bed, triangle bed
Hollyhock	Edible leaves and flowers, blossom	Edge bed
Honesty	Edible roots, blossom	Polyculture beds, long border, hedge
Hop (golden)	Edible early shoots	Hedge
Hosta, 2 varieties	Edible early leaves, floral	Polyculture beds
Japanese hardy ginger, (*Zingiber mioga*)	Edible early shoots	Polyculture beds
Japanese quince, (*Chaenomeles*)	Edible fruits	Triangle bed
Himalayan honeysuckle (*Leycesteria formosa*)	Edible fruits	Edge bed
Mallow	Edible leaves, blossom	Triangle bed
Nasturtium	Edible flowers, blossom	Polyculture beds
Primrose	Edible flowers, blossom	Hedge and edge bed
Solomon's seal, 2 varieties	Edible early shoots, floral	Triangle bed, long border
Wild plants		
Bird's-foot-trefoil	Blossom, nitrogen fixer	Triangle bed

Name	Benefits	Where
Bittercress	Edible, early blossom	Triangle bed, long border, hedge
Bluebell, wild	Blossom	Hedge
Brambles	Edible berries, blossom	Polyculture beds
Buttercup	Blossom	Polyculture bed, hedge
Campion	Blossom	Hedge
Cleavers		Hedge, long border
Clove root	Blossom	Hedge, edge bed
Clover	Blossom, nitrogen fixer	Lawn, long border
Common vetch	Blossom, nitrogen fixer	Triangle bed
Cow parsley	Blossom	Hedge
Dandelion	Edible flowers, blossom	All areas
Dead nettle	Blossom	Hedge
Dock	Deep rooted, brings up minerals	All areas
Foxglove[8]	Blossom	Long border, edge bed
Fumitory	Blossom	Long border
Greater celandine	Blossom	Edge bed
Ground ivy	Blossom	All areas
Hedge woundwort	Blossom	Edge bed
Herb robert	Blossom	Long border, edge bed, polyculture beds
Hogweed	Edible seeds, blossom	Hedge
Ivy	Wildlife value	Hedge
Meadowsweet	Blossom	Polyculture beds
Nettle	Wildlife value	Hedge, edge bed
Plantain	Has medicinal properties	Hedge, edge bed
Rosebay willowherb	Blossom	Edge bed
Scarlet pimpernel		Edge bed
Self heal	Blossom	Triangle bed, polyculture beds
Snowdrop, wild	Early blossom	Hedge, edge bed, triangle bed
Sow thistle	Blossom	Polyculture beds
Speedwell	Blossom	Triangle bed

---

[8] Foxglove is a beneficial plant for the garden ecosystem, but it is also poisonous to humans.

Name	Benefits	Where
St John's wort	Blossom	Triangle bed
Stitchwort	Floral	Hedge
Sweet woodruff	Blossom	Hedge
Toad flax	Blossom	Triangle bed
Tufted vetch	Blossom, nitrogen fixer	Triangle bed
Valerian	Blossom	Polyculture beds
Violets	Blossom	Polyculture beds, long border
Welsh poppy	Blossom	Edge bed
Wild rose	Blossom	Hedge
Wood sorrel	Edible, floral	Hedge
Yarrow	Blossom	Triangle bed, polyculture beds

Conventional garden flowers and shrubs

Name	Benefits	Where
Agapanthus	Floral	Long border
Alchemilla mollis	Floral	Edge bed, triangle bed
Alstroemeria	Floral	Long border
Astrantia	Floral	Long border
Aubretia	Blossom	Edge bed
Baptisia australis	Blossom, nitrogen fixer	Long border
Bee balm	Floral	Long border
Berberis	Blossom, berries for birds	Hedge
Broom	Nitrogen fixer, blossom	Hedge
Buddleia	Blossom	Hedge
Bugle	Floral	Edge bed
Catmint	Blossom	Edge bed
Chokeberry	Blossom, berries for birds	Long border
Comfrey, dwarf	Blossom	Polyculture beds
Cornus, 2 varieties		Hedge
Cotoneaster	Blossom, berries for birds	Hedge
Creeping Jenny	Blossom	Triangle bed, long border
Crocus	Floral	Edge bed
Cyclamen	Floral	Long border
Daffodils, 2 varieties	Floral	Polyculture beds, triangle bed
Flax, 2 varieties	Floral	Triangle bed, long border
Grape hyacinths	Floral	Edge bed

Name	Benefits	Where
Hebe	Blossom	Polyculture beds
Helichrysum	Floral	Polyculture beds
Hellebore	Floral	Long border
Japanese acer, 2 varieties		Long border, triangle bed
Lilac, dwarf variety	Blossom, fragrance	Long border
Lily, Martagon	Floral	Triangle bed
Love in a mist	Blossom	Long border
Lungwort	Blossom	Polyculture beds, edge bed
Lysimachia clethroides	Floral	Long border
Penstemon	Floral	Long border
Phacelia	Blossom	Long border, polyculture beds
Philadelphus, La Belle Etoile	Blossom, fragrance	Long border
Phlox	Blossom, fragrance	Triangle bed
Polemium	Floral	Long border
Pyracantha	Blossom, berries for birds	Hedge
Rose, 6 varieties	Floral, fragrance	Long border, triangle bed
Saxifrage	Floral	Edge bed
Scabious	Floral	Edge bed
Sedum, 3 varieties	Blossom	Triangle bed, polyculture beds
Thrift	Blossom	Edge bed
Viburnum opulus, (Guelder Rose)	Blossom, berries for birds	Hedge
Viburnum lantana, (Wayfaring Tree)	Blossom, berries for birds	Hedge
Winter jasmine	Winter flowers	Hedge
Trees and shrubs		
Ash		Hedge
Beech		Hedge
Blackthorn	Early blossom, fruit (sloes)	Hedge
Hawthorn	Early blossom, fruit (haws)	Hedge
Hazel	Nuts	Hedge
Holly	Early blossom, berries	Hedge
Leylandii		Hedge
Silver birch		Hedge
Sycamore		Hedge
Witch hazel	Early blossom	Hedge

appendix 2

discussion of David Holmgren's principles of permaculture

Forest gardening is often seen as one branch of the much broader topic of permaculture and because permaculture has its own guiding principles it has been suggested to me in the past that these give sufficient guidance for forest gardening. These permaculture principles are set out and explained in David Holmgren's book *Permaculture: Principles and Pathways Beyond Sustainability*. I love this book and find these principles totally compatible with my own thinking. However, permaculture principles are wide ranging and applicable to a huge number of contexts and to my mind they are not sufficiently focussed to describe how to interact with a forest garden. With this in mind here is a short summary of my thoughts on comparing Holmgren's principles with the work I have undertaken.

principle 1: observe and interact

Yes indeed forest gardening is all about observing and interacting. But you need much more detail about stopping, watching, waiting, doing nothing until you have to and then doing only the minimum.

principle 2: catch and store energy

Yes, indeed – biomass is the sun's energy caught in plants and then in all the animals that eat them – and it is supremely important to generating fertility in the forest garden, this is fundamental, but again needs more elaboration.

principle 3 : obtain a yield

Yes, subject to the caveat of harvesting only enough. It is not *all* about yield for people.

principle 4 : apply self-regulation and accept feedback

Yes, by continually watching with polyculture eyes and understanding with polyculture mind and making the context dependent decisions about what to do next (or not do next).

principle 5 : use and value renewable resources

Yes, everything in the forest garden is a renewable resource, in particular see life cycle gardening.

principle 6 : produce no waste

Yes, there is no such thing as waste in a forest garden.

principle 7 : design from pattern to detail

In Holmgren's work, pattern is an entire landscape and a forest garden is but a detail within that landscape. Permaculture also lays a lot of emphasis on designing in advance and, as I have explained in the text, this is one option. However, it doesn't suit everyone or every situation.

principle 8 : integrate rather than segregate

Yes, a polyculture and an ecosystem are all about integration. Becoming a different gardener is about the forest gardener integrating with the forest garden.

principle 9 : use small and slow solutions

Yes, everything is slow and solutions present themselves.

principle 10 : use and value diversity

Absolutely – biodiversity is one of the most important aspects of forest gardening.

principle 11 : use edges and value the marginal

Yes, what other people see as pests and weeds are certainly marginal, and, as described in chapter 12, they are as valued as any other part of the ecosystem.

principle 12 : creatively use and respond to change

Yes, with polyculture eyes and polyculture mind seeing what is going on and making context based decisions.

appendix 3

some thoughts on food growing on a larger scale

Forest gardening changes many things – it enables us to grow food, to restore and enliven the local ecosystem and at the same time brings us into a radically different relationship with the natural world, such that we are effectively embedded within nature and seeking to co-operate with it and not to control. Despite these benefits, forest gardening is not a panacea and I am not going to claim that it will feed the world or that it is the only way to help or restore the environment. There are farmers and growers all around the world exploring ways to ameliorate the harm done by contemporary farming, whilst growing commercially viable crops in ecologically appropriate ways. Such techniques may hold the potential to change our food growing from a destructive practice to a constructive one.

agroforestry

Forest gardening is often categorised as one amongst a set of techniques that fall within the broader designation of agroforestry. These techniques combine agricultural or horticultural crops with trees grown together for mutual benefit. Examples of agroforestry include forest farming, silvoarable (agricultural or horticultural crops grown alongside a tree crop), and silvopasture (trees integrated with grazing for domestic animals).

Forest farming is about growing high-value speciality crops in what is usually a modified, but pre-existing woodland. Potential crops include shiitake mushrooms grown on logs and medicinal or decorative plants growing under the tree canopy. This system modifies the local ecosystem but does not significantly interfere with it or its value as wildlife habitat. Silvopasture combines fruit, nut or nitrogen fixing trees with permanent pasture for animal forage. The trees provide the animals with shade and protection reducing mortality rates and improving productivity; it does, however, require careful management to protect trees from the animals.

Agroforestry is a definite move away from monocultural farming or forestry and it has been demonstrated to be more productive than these methods. Aside from their productivity, trees are permanent fixtures in the landscape over decades or even centuries. Their presence provides benefits to the local ecology and, the more integrated they can be with other land uses, the better.

regenerative agriculture

Regenerative agriculture is an approach to food and farming systems that regenerates topsoil and increases biodiversity. It seeks to integrate farming and the natural world to such an extent that their boundaries become indistinguishable. It does not permit the use of chemicals or other harmful agents and recognises that each farm is inextricably linked to the surrounding natural environment. Silvopasture and agroforestry systems fall within the definition of regenerative agriculture; and other techniques employed include mob and holistic planned livestock grazing, no-till cropping and the use of multi-species cover crops.

Masanobu Fukuoka's natural farming

Masanobu Fukuoka (1913 - 2008) was raised on a farm and then studied at agricultural college. He was working as a plant pathologist when he experienced a life changing personal crisis which culminated in him having a revelation of nature as perfect in and of itself. He left his scientific job and returned to the family farm where he then spent over 65 years developing and then perfecting what he called 'natural farming' – a way of growing healthy and productive crops that was completely integrated with how nature works. He did this by not doing the routine and accepted agricultural practices – he stopped ploughing, he grew rice plants in un-flooded fields, he spread straw to control weeds and he obtained two harvests each year by sowing barley seeds at the foot of the almost ripe rice plants, and vice versa. Mr Fukuoka also had an orchard – created not by design but by mixing up over a hundred different seeds into balls of clay and scattering them everywhere. It sounds very much like a forest garden.

> *There are deciduous and evergreen trees of all sizes growing together with shrubs, vegetables, berries and ground cover plants. A large apple tree nearby had ginger and wild onions growing near the base, a blueberry bush above them, kiwi growing on the branches of the tree and an akebia vine growing above the kiwi.* ~ Larry Korn, 2015

Regenerative agriculture and natural farming may or may not share any specific methods or practices, but they share an ethos of thinking and working as an inextricable part of the natural world.

acknowledgements

Nurturing and bringing a book to publication is a lengthy process and one which is supported – directly and indirectly – by all kinds of people and influences. I would like to offer my wholehearted appreciation:

Firstly to my garden of equal delights for everything I have learned there.

Then there are the intellectual influences from people – in person, in books and online. These are far too numerous to count, but they frame the context of my thinking and have sown seeds that stimulated fresh ideas to germinate. The most significant books and authors are mentioned in the text and bibliography.

My former university tutor from Aberystwyth, the late Dr Bill Edwards, remains a strong influence despite the passage of years. His 'Landscape and Locality' course was perhaps the first time I learned to look really closely at how humans shape and value the world we live in. The rigour of thought he exemplified and expected will always be with me.

My partner, Pat, travels with me on life's journey, in the garden and beyond. Her patience, encouragement and support make all the difference to everything.

And finally my thanks go to Andrew and Debbie at Triarchy Press for taking on this book and bringing it to fruition. Their professionalism, expertise and support have been outstanding.

about the author

Anni Kelsey grew up in the
suburbs of Reading at a time
when there were still
fragments of the natural
world left close by – woods,
a lake, tiny streams and a
few large trees – and when
children were allowed to
spend more time
unsupervised. Walking
everywhere in all weathers,
and spending much of her
free time playing outside,
gave her ample opportunity
to watch these slivers of nature and to fall in love with them.

In her late twenties she escaped to west Wales and immediately felt
very connected to the landscape, the people and the culture and took
the opportunity to study both geography and the Welsh language as
a mature student at Aberystwyth University. Circumstances took
her back across the border to the suburbs of Telford and, though she
would have loved to work out of doors, her employment consigned
her to a series of desks in many different workplaces.

Discovering forest gardening marked a significant turning point in
her life and she wrote *Edible Perennial Gardening* in 2014 as a
practical guide to growing perennial vegetables and polycultures.
When the opportunity arose to move back to Wales she seized it and
she now lives in the hilly border country of eastern Powys. Now
retired from employment you will often find her outside – in the
garden, the woods or out on the hills, or else tucked up somewhere
cosy reading a book!

bibliography

Anderson, M. Kat, 2005, *Tending the Wild*, University of California Press

Barstow, Stephen, 2014, *Around the World in 80 Plants*, Permanent Publications

Berry, Wendell, 2017, *The World Ending Fire*, ed. Paul Kingsnorth, Penguin Books

Buhner, Stephen Harrod, 2002, *The Lost Language of Plants*, Chelsea Green

Dark Mountain Project, 2017, *Walking on Lava, Selected Works for Uncivilised Times*, Chelsea Green

Eisenstein, Charles, 2013, *The More Beautiful World Our Hearts Know is Possible*, North Atlantic Books

Ford, Anabel and Nigh, Ronald, 2015, *The Maya Forest Garden – Eight Millennia of Sustainable Cultivation of the Tropical Woodlands*, Routledge

Fukuoka, Masanobu, 1978, *The One-Straw Revolution*, New York Review Books

Goulson, Dave, 2013, *A Sting in the Tale*, Vintage

Holmgren, David, 2011, *Permaculture: Principles and Pathways Beyond Sustainability*, Permanent Publications

Jacke, Dave and Toensmeier, Eric, 2005a, *Edible Forest Gardens Vol One: Ecological Vision and Theory for Temperate Climate Permaculture*, Chelsea Green

Jacke, Dave and Toensmeier, Eric, 2005b, *Edible Forest Gardens Vol Two: Ecological Design and Practice for Temperate Climate Permaculture*, Chelsea Green

Kelsey, Anni, 2014, *Edible Perennial Gardening*, Permanent Publications

Korn, Larry, 2015, *One-Straw Revolutionary, The Philosophy and Work of Masanobu Fukuoka*, Chelsea Green

Ralph, Ann, 2014, *Grow a Little Fruit Tree*, Storey Publishing

Remiarz, Tomas, 2017, *Forest Gardening in Practice*, Permanent Publications

Toensmeier, Eric, 2016, *The Carbon Farming Solution*, Chelsea Green

Tree, Isabella, 2018, *Wilding*, Picador

about Triarchy Press

Triarchy Press is an independent publisher of books that bring a systemic or contextual approach to many areas of life, including:

Government, Education, Health and other public services ~ Ecology and Regenerative Cultures ~ Leading and Managing Organisations ~ The Money System ~ Psychotherapy and other Expressive Therapies ~ Walking, Psychogeography and Mythogeography ~ Movement and Somatics ~ Innovation ~ The Future and Future Studies

Other related titles by Triarchy Press include:

* Designing Regenerative Cultures ~ **Daniel Christian Wahl**
* Small Arcs of Larger Circles ~ **Nora Bateson**
* Thrivability ~ **Jean M. Russell**
* Stone Talks ~ **Alyson Hallett**
* The Wisdom of Not-Knowing ~ **Bob Chisholm & Jeff Harrison**
* Guidebook for an Armchair Pilgrimage ~ **John Schott, Phil Smith & Tony Whitehead**
* Arranged by Flowers ~ **Miss Padget**

For more details, and to purchase any of these titles, visit:

www.triarchypress.net